Quiet Moments in The Villages

A Treasure Hunt Devotional

DORIS HOOVER

Mark,

Thank you for your touching
endorsement. I my book will
be a blessing to you.
Peace + joy,
Doris

"Every once in a great while, one reads a devotion that connects the beauty and gift of nature in a heart deep, Christ-centered way. Doris has written that kind of a book! Her transparency and passion will nourish your mind and soul. This is a remarkable book written by a remarkable woman!"

Terri Kane, Celebrate Recovery Leader and E-News Editor
Mt. Laurel, New Jersey

"You don't need to live in The Villages to love these devotions. Through her reflections on nature, Doris Hoover draws you closer to God's Presence, His Compassion, His Love, and more. You'll want to read these inspiring words again and again."

Delores Kight, Co-president
Ocala chapter of Word Weavers International

"Obviously captivated by the stunning beauty of God's creation, Doris Hoover has drawn us into her world of imagination. Walk with her through these beautiful scenes of nature in The Villages, Florida as she shares her insights into God's Word through these inspirational devotions."

Mark Fessler, Minister of Fairway Christian Church

Quiet Moments in The Villages: A Treasure Hunt Devotional

Copyright © 2016 Doris Hoover

Editor: Natalie Gillespie
Cover photograph by Ron Clark, The Villages, FL
used with permission.
Cover design: Bob Ousnamer
Page layout design: Dawn Staymates

ISBN: 978-1-941733-31-8

Published by EA Books Publishing a division of
Living Parables of Central Florida, Inc. a 501c3
Eabookspublishing.com

Dedication

For the One who captivates my heart.

Table of Contents

Acknowledgements

I give enormous thanks to my husband Tim who encouraged me to follow my dream. He went above and beyond in supporting my efforts. I love you always.

I want to thank my Word Weavers group, especially Delores, Linda and Marian, who read and critiqued my work. Your inspiration, encouragement and support are priceless.

I wish abundant blessings upon the many friends and family members whose stories enriched my messages.

A special thanks to my editor Natalie and the production team at EA Books Publishing. Your expertise made this book a reality.

Introduction

In the busyness of our lives, we tend to miss the subtle messages our Creator leaves along our paths. He reveals himself through the things he's made. The Villages has many beautiful spaces which invite quiet reflection. These places inspire me and stir my heart to search for deeper spiritual lessons. This book is my way of sharing the amazing things the Lord taught me as I tuned into the natural world around me.

I call this book "A Treasure Hunt Devotional" because you can go on a treasure hunt to discover the very places that inspired me. As you visit each location, let your senses soak in the beauty of nature. Feel the Lord reaching out to you. When you begin to uncover God's presence all around you, you will begin to experience the greatest treasure of all.

Although my messages were inspired by various locations in The Villages, the topics are universal and speak to needs we all have. The beauty of nature exists everywhere. *Quiet Moments in The Villages* was written for both Villagers and people living outside of The Villages. As you read this book, I hope you'll become more sensitive to God's presence in nature, and as a result, draw closer to our awesome Creator.

Doris Hoover

Laurel Manor Recreation Center

One

A New Song

"Neither do I condemn you. Go your way. From now on, sin no more"
(John 8:11 WEB).

Beneath the covered portico of Laurel Manor Recreation Center, I sit and listen to birds serenading from the treetops. Their songs float over me in joyous tunes. Their singing reminds me my life is the melody I make for God.

Over the years, inconsistency and imperfection marred my life's melody. Simple joys and happy times added layers of sweet harmony. However, trauma and trials brought dissonance and discordance. There were periods of time when the track of my life played totally out of tune with the composition God wrote for me.

When my life was nothing more than objectionable noise, the Savior called to me. He held me in his arms and kissed my head. He reminded me that together we could create beautiful music. The Lord forgave my off-key notes. He gave me a chance to rewrite my song as a duet we could sing together. The Savior gave me a chance to write a new song with my life.

One day, while Jesus taught in the temple courts, he gave the same opportunity to a woman. A group of men dragged her into the temple courts. They stood her in the middle of the crowd, telling Jesus she had been caught in the act of adultery. They were testing Jesus to see if he would support the Law by saying she should be stoned. As the crowd jeered and pointed at the woman, Jesus knelt down and began to write in the sand. The crowd persisted, demanding he address the situation. Jesus stood up and responded, "Let any one of you who is without sin be the first to throw a stone at her" (John 8:7 NIV). Then Jesus stooped back down. He didn't stare at the crowd daring them to throw stones. Instead, Jesus looked at the ground, giving the people time to

2

reflect upon their actions. He allowed those gathered in the crowd time to examine their own lives.

One by one, her accusers left until only Jesus and the woman remained. The Lord didn't look at the woman in disgust. He stood up and asked, "Woman, where are your accusers? Did no one condemn you?"

"No one, Lord."

Jesus said, "Neither do I condemn you. Go your way. From now on, sin no more" (John 8:10-11 WEB). Jesus gave the woman a chance to compose a new song with her life.

The Apostle Peter had a time when his life went terribly off-key. He was one of the twelve chosen disciples who accompanied Jesus everywhere. When he boasted of his faithfulness, Jesus told him the day would come when three times Peter would deny knowing the Lord.

That day came when Jesus was arrested and taken to the High Priest. Peter followed behind the crowd, trying to remain inconspicuous. Several times, people asked him if he was one of Jesus' followers. Peter claimed he wasn't. "Then he began to swear, 'I don't know the man!'" (Matthew 26:74 WEB). With his third denial, Peter remembered the Lord's earlier prediction. Peter ran from the crowd crying bitterly. He had denied knowing the Christ. Was there any hope for him?

After the resurrection, before ascending to heaven, Jesus found Peter. Not once, not twice, but three times, Jesus asked Peter to take care of the sheep, referring to the new converts. The Lord's request gave Peter a chance to erase his three discordant notes and compose a new song by carrying out the plan Jesus had for him.

God listens for a sweet melody to flow from our lives. Too often, our life songs become off-key ballads. Our pure tones get scratchy in the dissonance of our flesh. Rather than condemning us for our bad choices, the Lord offers us a chance to create a new song. He offers to help us compose a song that resounds with notes of grace and mercy.

O Lord, we desire to change our discordant lives into beautiful melodies that float up to you.

It's not too late, precious one. Together we'll compose a glorious symphony.

A MOMENT OF REFLECTION

What kind of music is your life playing for God? Jesus can help you compose a delightful duet. Write down one thing you're willing to change.

Town Square Spanish Springs Fountain

Two

Unending Streams

"And again they cried unto thee, and thou heardest from the heavens,
and many times didst thou deliver them, according to thy mercies"
(Nehemiah 9:28 DARBY).

Gentle splashing draws me to a fountain where streams of water spray into a pool. The sound of flowing water soothes me. It reminds me that God's mercy is like unending streams, flowing with second chances.

The Israelites experienced God's mercy. Time and again, they wandered away from the Father's teachings, refusing to listen or obey. They forgot about the many miracles God had performed among them. As a consequence, they suffered captivity by foreign nations.

After being released from a time of captivity, Israel returned home to find the walls of Jerusalem broken down and the gates burned. When the Old Testament prophet Nehemiah learned of the destruction, he wept. He confessed the sins he and the people had committed against the Lord. He begged God to show compassion upon the people. Then Nehemiah led the people in rebuilding the city walls.

Upon completion, Nehemiah gathered the people together to listen as Ezra the priest read from the Book of Law. He read it out loud from sunrise until noon. The people listened with full attention. They repented before the Lord as Ezra reminded them of the many times God had been patient and longsuffering toward them. Even though they had repeatedly wandered away from the Lord's teachings, refusing to listen to him or to obey his words, the Lord's streams of mercy never ceased.

The Lord loved them in spite of their human weaknesses. Each time they begged for the Lord to show compassion and mercy, he gave them another chance. When Ezra finished reading the Book of Law, the people declared the Lord had been just and acted faithfully; they had done wrong. The people promised to be faithful and obey God's commands. The Lord responded to their remorse with patience and compassion. His mercy was like an unending stream.

We learn about unending streams of patience and compassion when we become parents. As we spend time with little ones, we find ourselves repeating the same instructions and teaching the same lessons all day long. *Remember to wash your hands. We don't run in the house. Take turns and share. Say "please" and "thank you."* We feel like a broken record, and we wonder if the children will ever remember the rules on their own. But, because we love them, our patience and compassion is limitless.

Once our children become teenagers and young adults, we learn even more about compassion. As we watch our children navigate the complexities of life, we want them to succeed. It hurts us to see them stumble and fall. We want to pick them up, but they have to get up on their own. We cheer for them. We pray for them. We never give up on them, even when they break our hearts. We always want them to have another chance to get it right. That is the essence of compassion and mercy.

Jesus showed unending streams of mercy toward his enemies. As he hung on the cross, they mocked him and tormented him. Jesus responded by asking God to forgive them because they didn't understand what they were doing.

Now, Jesus intercedes on our behalf, reminding the Father to be merciful to us. Our Heavenly Father looks upon us with a heart filled with patience and longsuffering. When we humbly ask for forgiveness, the Lord opens his arms and draws us to his breast. He doesn't accuse us. He forgives us. Our loving Father scoops us up and whispers words of love. Each time we approach our Lord with tears of regret, he embraces us with arms full of mercy. As many times as we repent, our Lord forgives us. We can never deplete God's abundance of love. His mercy flows over us in ceaseless streams of second chances.

O Lord, we are desperate for your unending streams of mercy.

Precious one, my love for you is never-ending.

A MOMENT OF REFLECTION

During what times in your life has the Lord given you a second chance to get it right? Write about them.

View of Bonifay Course

Three

The Colors of God's Touch

"To give them a crown for ashes, the oil of joy for mourning, a garment of praise for the spirit of grief" (Isaiah 61:3 DRA).

A red-winged blackbird sails past me, wings spread wide, a crimson stripe blazing against its onyx feathers. My breath catches. Standing beneath the trees near Bonifay Golf Course, I realize I'm beholding the amazing colors of God's touch in nature.

The Lord also touches our lives and colors them with beauty. I beheld the colors of God's touch in my life. I went through a time when each day was gray. Somber colors cloaked my spirit when unforeseen circumstances broke my heart. In my sadness, I called out to the Lord for comfort. I read my Bible, searching for answers. As I soaked up Scripture, I realized the Lord was present in my circumstances. He heard my sobbing and he felt my hurt. My Heavenly Father offered his shoulder for my tears.

The Lord lifted me from my ashy corner and brushed me off. With a gentle touch, he sprinkled golden flecks of joy over my sadness. He turned my despair to praise. When I look back through my memories of that time, instead of gray I see the shining color of hope. The Lord healed my hurt. He was the blue sky breaking through my clouds.

Hagar and Sarai were women in the Old Testament who knew sorrow but experienced the colors of God's touch. Because she was barren, Sarai decided to give her husband children through her servant Hagar. Hagar conceived and began to despise her mistress. Sarai regretted giving Hagar to her husband. Sarai's days were gray with sadness and green with jealousy. She mistreated Hagar so harshly that Hagar fled to the desert.

10

An angel found Hagar sitting by a spring in the desert. The angel promised Hagar she would bear a son who would become a great nation. The child would be called Ishmael, meaning God hears, "because the Lord has heard thy affliction" (Genesis16:11 DRA). Hagar's misery brightened to the color of joy. She returned home and gave birth to Ishmael.

Meanwhile, God changed Sarai's name to Sarah, princess of many, and Abram's to Abraham, father of many. Soon, Sarah's life also turned bright. She no longer sat in the ashes of shame over being barren. She wore a crown of motherhood. The Lord touched her life with the sparkling color of triumph. She bore a son and named him Isaac.

During a celebration honoring Isaac, Ishmael mocked his younger half-brother. Sarah demanded Abraham send Hagar and Ishmael away. Once again, Hagar's world became dark. She wandered in the desert until her food and drink ran out. Then Hagar sat Ishmael under a tree while she went a distance away and sobbed because she and her son were going to die. The Lord heard her crying and opened her eyes to see a well of water. Hagar and Ishmael lived and prospered in the desert. Because of the Lord's touch, Hagar's life became colored with golden shades of joy.

Both Sarah and Hagar experienced sorrow, but the Lord turned their mourning to joy and their grief to praise. Each time their lives darkened, the Lord touched Sarah and Hagar with vivid Technicolor miracles that revived their spirits. He responded to their cries with beautiful brush strokes of compassion.

The Lord hears our cries also. He doesn't leave us in the ashes. He reaches out to us, lifts us up, and comforts us. God reaches down to touch our lives with goodness. He infuses our darkest moments with soothing hues. When we call to him, he pours cool blue streams into the crevices of our arid souls. He bathes us in lavender, calming our anxious thoughts. With crimson passion, the Lord's love floods our hearts. The touch of Jesus lifts us from the ashes and crowns our heads with the brilliant jewels of victory.

The blackbird spreads its wings to reveal God's touch on its feathers. We open up our memories to see the amazing colors of God's touch in our lives.

Heavenly Father, we cherish your touch.

My Precious child, your life reflects the colors of me.

A MOMENT OF REFLECTION

What colors has the Lord painted into your life? Write about them.

Doris Hoover

Sharon Rose Wiechens Preserve

Four

Back to Nature

"But the hour comes, and now is, when the true worshipers will worship the Father in spirit and truth, for the Father seeks such to be his worshipers" (John 4:23 WEB).

Fish, turtles, and frogs laze among the swampy grasses. Cranes wade along the water's edge, stalking their prey, and alligators slink through the mud. In this natural marshland, each creature finds a habitat to suit its needs.

This Nature Preserve is not man-made; it is God-made. Each creature's habitat is made according to God's perfect plan. The Lord also has a perfect plan for those who worship him. His plan is made clear to us through his Word.

In John 4, Jesus spoke with a Samaritan woman who followed the man-made traditions of her fathers. They worshipped on a mountain in Samaria. The woman was confused because the Jews worshipped in Jerusalem. She didn't know if both places were acceptable places of worship. Jesus went to the heart of the matter. He told the woman God desires worship that doesn't happen in a physical location; rather, it happens in a person's spirit. Jesus went on to explain that God's true worshipers worship him in spirit and in truth. These are the kinds of worshipers the Father desires.

There are many types of churches available to us. The variety of religions may confuse us in the same way the Samaritan woman was confused. We may wonder if it's possible for people from so many religious origins to please God with their worship.

I believe it is possible if we go "back to nature," back to the pure truth. "Every scripture [is] divinely inspired, and profitable for teaching, for conviction, for correction, for instruction in righteousness; that the man of God may be complete, fully fitted to every good work" (2 Timothy 3:16-17 DARBY).

When I became a new Christian, I attended a Sunday school class taught by a man who had a strong faith. He believed the Bible was God's letter to us. He challenged the class to study the Bible and consider it the cornerstone of anything we were taught. He told us to weigh everything we heard, whether from him, from preachers, or from other religious teachers, against what the Bible said. If there was a discrepancy, then we should go to the Bible to find the truth. Thanks to that righteous man, I diligently studied my Bible. To this day, I hold the Bible up as God's word to man. I value it above the words of any religious leader.

Jesus referred to himself as the Word. He claimed his words were eternal and they would never pass away. Peter understood the value of Jesus's words. He said, "Lord, to whom would we go? You have the words of eternal life" (John 6:68 WEB).

Pure truth is found in the Bible. It's the truth God reveals to us as an instruction book to teach us everything we need to know. When we step away from man-made buildings and man-made traditions and base our beliefs solely on God's word, we will discover God-made worship.

The kind of worship our Father desires originates in the pure truth of the Bible and deep in our spirits. It's an intimate worship between us and our Creator.

Spending quiet time in places God created draws us closer to him. There's something about nature that puts everything into perspective. We realize we are just a small part of the universe, and someone much greater than us created it. Our Creator gave us his words so we could know him. When we get back to the natural truth in the Bible, we'll be able to hear God's voice above all the confusion in the world.

O Lord, we desire to worship you in truth with our whole heart.

Precious child, I am the truth. Seek only me.

A MOMENT OF REFLECTION

Have you made a commitment to study the Bible so you can know the pure truth? Write down an action plan to get started.

Main Street in Brownwood

Five

Towering Palms

"The fear of Jehovah is clean, enduring forever: The ordinances of Jehovah are true, and righteous altogether. More to be desired are they than gold, yea, than much fine gold; Sweeter also than honey and the droppings of the honeycomb. Moreover by them is thy servant warned; in keeping them there is great reward" (Psalm 19:9-11 ASV).

Canary Island date palm trees line Main Street in Brownwood. They tower over the walkway like mighty kings, standing majestically beneath crowns of leaves and commanding respect by their awesome presence.

I am reminded that God's word towers along the pathway of our lives, commanding respect because the message comes from the King of Heaven. Our Creator gives us ordinances to light our way. They are sure and righteous precepts given to guide our steps. They're majestic because they originate in the mind of God.

After Israel escaped captivity from Egypt, the Lord God gave the nation ordinances to follow. He gave them wise and righteous laws to guide their lives. The laws would distinguish Israel from the other people on earth, setting them apart as God's chosen people.

In order to give the law, the Lord told Moses to meet with him on the top of Mount Sinai. Three days before the appointed meeting, the people purified themselves. Boundaries were established at the foot of the mountain. Anyone crossing the boundary line was to be put to death.

On the third day, thunder rumbled and lightning flashed as a dense cloud covered the mountain. With the sound of a loud trumpet blast, Moses led the people to the base of the mountain, then he climbed to the top. The Lord descended in fire. The mountain shook and billowed with smoke. The people were terrified.

God spoke to Moses, giving him the words that became known as The Law. Included in The Law were the Ten Commandments and the ordinances by which the nation of Israel was to live. When Moses came down from the mountain and told the people all the Lord's words and his laws, they responded unanimously, "All the words which Jehovah hath spoken we will do" (Exodus 24:3 ASV).

Later, in the New Testament, we see how Jesus revered God's word. Before beginning his ministry, Jesus was led by the Spirit into the desert where he was tempted by the devil. Satan even used God's words in his temptations, trying to trick Jesus. In response to each temptation, Jesus replied, "It is written..." (Matthew 4:4 ASV). Jesus answered Satan by using the very words that had been passed down through each generation since the time Moses received them on Mount Sinai. God's word was Jesus' power over temptation. It towered above Satan's cunning ways.

In the book of Hebrews, we read, "For the word of God is living and active, and sharper than any two-edged sword, and piercing even to the dividing of soul and spirit, of both joints and marrow, and quick to discern the thoughts and intents of the heart" (Hebrews 4:12 ASV). The words in the Bible are living words given to us from the mind of our Creator. They instruct us in righteous living. They make us wise.

Although The Law was given specifically to Israel, we have the Bible to guide us. We have the whole story of God's plan for mankind. The Bible opens with the story of creation and the origin of man. It proceeds with the history of chosen individuals and then with the history of a chosen nation. The Bible introduces us to Jesus and his ministry. We read about God's plan to redeem sinful men. In the letters to the churches, we receive instructions on Christian living. The Bible closes with a prophecy about the end of this world and a glimpse of Heaven. There is no book more valuable to man than the book given to us by our Heavenly Father. It contains divinely inspired words.

The Lord's words are more precious than gold and sweeter than honey. They enrich our lives. The words of the King of Heaven are like towering palms guiding us along the right path.

Heavenly Father, may your precepts tower above all else.

Precious child, treasure my word in your heart.

A MOMENT OF REFLECTION

What are some of your favorite Scripture verses? Write a couple of them here and commit them to memory.

Flower Garden

Six

Mornings by the Garden

"And the Lord God took the man, and put him into the garden of Eden to dress it and to keep it" (Genesis 2:15 KJV).

In the coolness of early morning, gardens awaken and stretch toward the sun. Like sleepy eyes opening to the light, flowers unfurl their petals. Roses stand up to smooth their ruffled skirts and mist the air with a sweet fragrance. I love to begin my day by the garden. My heart skips a beat as I gaze upon the exotic colors.

Then I think about another garden. The Garden of Eden must have been the loveliest place ever created. God's artistic majesty must have been showcased in the flora and fauna. I can only imagine the stunning flowers that grew in the Garden of Eden. The Lord's splendor bloomed in the plants as he nourished them with sunshine and watered them with dew.

Then God placed man in the lush garden to tend it. Adam and Eve lived in a place of perfection. Not only was the environment glorious, but also they had the privilege of being with God. The book of Genesis tells us the Lord God walked in the garden in the cool of day and he spoke with Adam and Eve. They had the honor of communing with their Creator face-to-face.

There is something about face-to-face communication that creates a special bond. When I was in middle school, I had a close friend named Marie. We walked and talked all the time. We laughed, shared secrets, and encouraged one another through our early teen challenges. We helped each other survive those confusing years. Then her family moved away during high school. We wrote letters, but it wasn't the same as being together walking and talking.

Even though the Lord doesn't walk on earth today, he wants to commune with us. He has always reached out to mankind and his Presence has always been with us in some form. In the Old Testament, God spoke directly to the prophets who made his words known to everyone else. While Israel wandered in the wilderness, the Lord's Presence dwelt among the people as they journeyed to the Promised Land.

During New Testament times, God dwelt on earth in the form of Jesus. The Apostles walked and talked with Jesus daily, discussing spiritual matters and learning from him.

After the resurrection of Christ, the Holy Spirit was sent to abide with men. Today, Christians commune with the Father through the Holy Spirit who dwells in our hearts. We've never been alone on earth. Our Creator has always communed with us in one form or another.

I discovered the wonderful experience of close communion with God. Although I'd been a Christian for many years, it was during a time of despair that I experienced deep intimacy with my Savior. The Lord walked close by my side. I bonded with my loving Savior at a deep emotional level. He became my best friend. His Presence encompassed me. He was the last one I spoke to at night and the first one I spoke to each morning. I thrived in his constant closeness. I long for the day when I'll see my Lord's face, when I can touch him and sit on his lap and feel his arms around me.

Even though we can't yet see God face-to-face, we can know him with all of our hearts. We can't see him walking in the Garden of Eden like Adam and Eve did, but we can see his fingerprints on every bloom in our own gardens. We inhale his essence wafting from the flowers. In the colors and shapes of plants, we glimpse the magnificence of our Creator's mind. We experience his provision in fruits, vegetables, and herbs.

A garden reveals much about our Heavenly Father. It's the perfect place to feel close to him. We sense his whispers in the breeze. We feel his warmth in every sunbeam.

O Lord, we come to the garden to seek you.

Come, my child, walk and talk with me.

A MOMENT OF REFLECTION

Look around you at the beauty of nature. Walk slowly, sensing every aspect of nature—its smells, sounds, sights and feelings. Let your spirit connect with God's Spirit and carry on a conversation in your heart. Listen for his response.

Butterfly Chair at Hospice House

Seven

A Butterfly Life

"Therefore, don't be anxious for tomorrow, for tomorrow will be anxious for itself" (Matthew 6:34 WEB).

A Monarch butterfly flitted about the wrought iron butterfly chair, alighting on a flower. Then it lifted on the breeze and fluttered to another. The butterfly seemed so light and carefree. I got lost in its happy world.

I wasn't at the Hospice House to visit a loved one, I was just sitting in the butterfly chair thinking about life and butterflies. I was enchanted by their graceful fluttering movement. They seemed to be dancing on air currents, as though they didn't have a care in the world.

I'd love to feel as weightless as those fluttering beauties, but sometimes worry weighs me down until I feel more like a slug than a butterfly. The Bible tells me to cast my cares on the Lord, but when I trudge beneath a burden of worries, I forget to look up. I become consumed with my burden.

Jesus discusses how pointless it is to worry. "Which of you by being anxious, can add one moment to his lifespan?" (Matthew 6:27 WEB). Jesus tells us to look at the birds. They don't worry because they rely totally on God to provide food for them. They don't plant or harvest crops, but they have food to eat.

We never see birds huddled together worrying about their next meal. They don't sit despondently on branches moaning. They seem as happy and unburdened as butterflies. Flying from tree to tree, they sing delightful melodies. Apparently, birds understand the secret of a worry-free life. They rely on one greater than themselves. Birds rely on their Creator to care for them. They may not be highly intelligent creatures, but they understand more about trust than I do.

Certainly, you and I carry legitimate burdens. We face complex issues, but the Lord doesn't want us to be weighed down by them. He doesn't want us to mull over them. We aren't supposed to analyze our problems from every angle, considering the various scenarios that could play out. It's a waste of energy to dwell on things we can't control. Not only is worry a waste of energy, but also it shows a lack of trust in our Heavenly Father.

When the health or loss of a loved one looms over us, the intensity of our worry compounds. But we're powerless to do anything about the situation. Our insides churn and our legs grow weak. Anxiety grips us as we imagine what lies ahead. We dread what the future may hold.

The Lord wants us to look at him, not focus on our grim scenarios.

The future is not part of our realm of concern. We can't control what happens in the present, let alone the future. Only the One who holds the future has power over it. When worries weigh heavily upon our hearts, the Lord asks us to hand them over to him. Through prayer, he provides a pathway that allows us to release our concerns to him. Worry doesn't cause change, but prayer does. The object of prayer is to bring us peace. When we're willing to entrust our worries to the Lord, he gives us peace. We can go through our days feeling lighter because we know the Lord is sharing our worries.

I thought about the power of prayer as I rested in the chair. With butterflies dancing past me and birds singing from the trees, I closed my eyes and prayed. I asked the Lord to take care of everything that weighed me down. As I leaned into his warmth, my lungs expanded and I breathed deeply. My neck and shoulders released their tension. Soon, my spirit felt as light as that butterfly dancing on the breeze.

O Lord, help us to let go of our burdens and to trust you with our cares.

Precious one, give your worries to me and I will lift you up.

A MOMENT OF REFLECTION

Write down everything you're worried about today. Lift up each concern in prayer and let the peace of the Lord wash over you.

MVP Athletic Club Courtyard Garden

Eight

An Oasis for the Weary

"For you have been a stronghold to the poor, a stronghold to the needy in his distress, a refuge from the storm, a shade from the heat" (Isaiah 25:4 WEB).

Pastel flowers, snapdragons and azaleas lounge around the perimeter of a peaceful courtyard. In the center, a fountain skims liquid music over it edges and the flowers sway to its melody. This tranquil courtyard is like an oasis of rest, a quiet nook apart from the bustling activity of Town Square.

Sometimes, life becomes so hectic we need to retreat to a calm quiet place where we can regroup. Sometimes, life's circumstances exhaust us and we need renewal.

The prophet Elijah needed a refuge, a place of safety. He was hated by Ahab the king of Israel, a king who did more evil in the eyes of the Lord than any king before him. King Ahab and Queen Jezebel worshipped the idol Baal, so God sent the prophet Elijah to Ahab with a message: There would be a severe drought upon the land because of Ahab's sins. After delivering the message, Elijah hid by a brook where God protected him from Ahab and the drought. The Lord's care was an oasis for Elijah. When the brook dried up, God provided an oasis for Elijah in the home of a widow. The Lord supplied them with food and water during the severe famine.

After three years of drought and famine, God sent Elijah back to Ahab to remind him that his wicked ways had brought this trouble upon Israel. Elijah challenged the prophets of Baal to call upon their god to send rain. They built an altar, offered sacrifices, and called upon Baal from morning until noon. Their god was as silent as a piece of wood. Then Elijah called upon the God of

Heaven. The Lord performed a miracle so the people could see he was the one true God. They bowed down before the Lord and he refreshed the land with rain.

Despite the miracles he witnessed, Ahab wouldn't repent. He went home and reported all that happened to Jezebel. She sent a message to Elijah, threatening to take his life.

Elijah fled to the desert again. Defeated and hopeless, he collapsed beneath a tree. God sent an angel to refresh Elijah with bread and water. Then the angel hid Elijah in a cave where he would be safe. God's faithful care was once again an oasis for the weary prophet.

Our Loving Father desires to be an oasis for us when we face discouragement, loneliness, fear or confusion. He desires to comfort and refresh us.

My friend Jenny married a career military man. Every few years she had to uproot her life and move to an unknown place. She had to find a new house, a new school for her children, a new church and new friends. She did all this without family nearby to help her. Each move filled her with anxiety.

Jenny found sanctuary in the quiet of her closet. That small space became an oasis where she sought the Lord and hid from the demands of moving. As she prayed for strength, the Lord held her and comforted her. He calmed her fears while breathing confidence into her spirit. One shaky step at a time, my friend held onto the Lord's hand as she settled herself and her family into their new home. With each move, the God of comfort refreshed her when she retreated into the oasis of his presence.

Just as the Lord helped Elijah and Jenny, he reaches out to us when we're overwhelmed by circumstances. When we feel too weak to go on, the Lord lifts us into his arms and refreshes our weary spirits. He invites us to rest in him until we regain our strength. Our Heavenly Father is our refuge and oasis.

O Lord, we come to you for renewal.

Precious one, I will revive you. Rest in my presence.

A MOMENT OF REFLECTION

When was there a time in your life when you took refuge in the Lord? Write a prayer thanking him for the comfort and refreshment he provided.

Pond in the Village of Charlotte

Nine

A Gentle Whisper

"And after the earthquake, a fire: Jehovah was not in the fire. And after the fire, a soft gentle voice" (1 Kings 19:12 DARBY).

I'm thankful for this quiet moment by the pond. Birds bob on the water like gently rocking feather buoys. Great egrets tiptoe along the shoreline. In this tranquil setting, I sit still and listen for God's soft gentle voice.

The Lord gave us the ability to experience quiet. God designed our ears with a limited hearing range, which allows us to experience moments of silence. When it's quiet, we tune into sounds we miss when it's noisy. It's during these moments we can hear God's gentle whisper.

Elijah couldn't hear the Lord's soft voice because he was listening to the noise of Ahab and Jezebel who wanted him dead. When the Lord found Elijah, he was hiding in a cave. The Lord asked Elijah what he was doing there. Elijah replied that he had been zealous to carry out the Lord's instructions, but the Israelites rejected him and God's covenant. Elijah claimed to be the only one left who bowed before the Most High God. The Lord told Elijah to get out of the cave and stand on the mountain as he passed by.

At first, there was a powerful wind that tore the mountains apart and shattered rocks. Elijah didn't see the Lord in the powerful wind. Then there was an earthquake and a fire, but the Lord wasn't in them either. Finally, after the fire came a gentle whisper. Elijah heard the whisper and stepped out of the cave. He recognized the still, small voice as the Presence of God. The Lord assured Elijah there were 7,000 others who had not bowed to Baal. He told Elijah to go back the way he had come because there was still work for him to complete.

The noise of life tends to distract us from the quiet of the Lord's presence. Then, like Elijah, we misjudge our circumstances and see them as worse than they are. Recently, my friend Lucy went through a frightening time. Her granddaughter was hospitalized with an unknown illness. The doctors couldn't figure out what was causing her problem. Lucy regularly sent updates to those who were praying. Each update revealed her confidence that the Lord was in control. Day after day, doctors brought bad news. It seemed that every strategy the medical experts tried didn't help. For months, her granddaughter was confined to a hospital bed, barely able to eat. In the midst of the noise of nurses and doctors and bad reports, Lucy sought the quiet of the Lord's presence and listened for his gentle whisper. As doubts and fears swished through her mind, she heard the Lord assuring her that she could trust him with her granddaughter. Finally, there was a breakthrough. The doctors pinpointed the problem. After months of hospitalization, her granddaughter was well enough to go home.

Every day Lucy spent in the hospital, she heard much noise. The wind shattered rocks when she learned of her granddaughter's illness. The earth quaked with each bad report. Fire roared in the unanswered questions. Still, despite all the noisy chaos around her, she could distinguish the quiet whisper of the Lord's voice. She could hear it because she knew his voice.

Babies recognize the sound of their mother's voice while in utero. Surrounded by the noise of pulsing blood and a pounding heartbeat, when they hear their mother's voice, their heart rates slow. In the same way, those who know the Lord recognize his voice, and in the midst of chaos it calms them.

When we quiet our spirits, the Lord's voice penetrates the noise around us and reaches our hearts. His gentle whispers remind us of his presence and bring clarity to our confusion. Even when we don't know the outcome of a frightening situation, we know the One who controls the situation. We trust the One with the soft, gentle voice.

Dear Lord, help us to still our spirits so we can hear you speaking.

Little one, listen for my voice. I am always near.

A MOMENT OF REFLECTION

Think of a time you heard the Lord's whisper above the noise of your life. Write down the message you received from him.

Odell Recreation Center

Ten

A Royal Heritage

"But you are a chosen people, a royal priesthood, a holy nation, a people for God's own possession, that you may proclaim the excellence of him who called you out of darkness into his wonderful light" (1 Peter 2:9 WEB).

Filtered sunlight sprinkles over me as I lounge beneath the pergola at Odell Pool. Overhead, palm branches shudder in the light breeze. I feel like an African queen languishing on my jungle throne, fanned by palm fronds.

Although my queenly status is merely a daydream, my royal heritage is real. I did nothing to merit it. My royalty came with a simple invitation from the King of Heaven. While I was damaged and unworthy, Jesus extended an invitation for me to become part of his family. Why did he want me? Why does he want you? Simple. Because he loves us. There is nothing in us deserving his gracious gift, but he offers it anyway.

When I accepted the invitation, Jesus welcomed me with open arms, as if he'd been waiting a long time for me to come home. He embraced my sin-encrusted soul, filthy from years of wandering in the world. He washed away the grime of my past and I became clean. He made my crimson stains as white as freshly washed wool. I was born again to become a new creature in Christ—unsoiled, holy and righteous. I became part of the family of God. I became a princess of the King of Kings.

In the fifteenth chapter of Luke, we read a parable Jesus told about the prodigal son, a young man who went astray. After asking his father for his share of the estate, he left home. He went to a distant land and squandered the money on wild living until there was nothing left. After a short while, there was a severe famine in the land. The young man had to hire himself out to a farmer who sent him to feed the pigs. The man was so hungry, he coveted the food he fed the pigs. Starving, the young man came to his senses. He decided to return home and ask his father for forgiveness, hoping he could at least be hired as a servant on his father's farm.

His father saw him in the distance and was filled with compassion. He ran to his son and embraced him and kissed him. He dressed the young man in the best robe and put a ring on his finger and sandals on his feet. He celebrated his son's return with a grand party, declaring, "for this, my son, was dead, and is alive again. He was lost, and is found" (Luke 15:24 WEB).

This story reveals the amazing love a father has for his child. It is an example of the love our Heavenly Father has for us. The Lord reaches for us while we're dirty with sins. He offers to wash away the soil of our worldly lives if we will accept his invitation. Just as the earthly father yearned for his prodigal son to return home, so the Lord reaches out to us, yearning for us to return to him, to run into the arms that long to hold us.

Jesus knocks on the door of our hearts hoping we will invite him into our lives. He waits like the father of the prodigal son. If we choose to open our lives to him, the angels in heaven have a grand celebration as our Heavenly Father proclaims, "This child of mine was lost and has been found!" The Lord opens the door of his kingdom and invites us to enter. He adopts us into his family and we become children of the King. We receive the unmerited gift of a royal heritage.

Maybe you're already a child of the King, but you have loved ones who have wandered from home. Don't be discouraged. We can pray for our prodigals and let them know they are loved no matter what. The prodigal son came to his senses. I found my way home from my wanderings in the world. There is always hope.

Father, who are we that we should be called your children?

You are precious in my sight, and I choose you.

A MOMENT OF REFLECTION

When did you accept the invitation to claim your royal heritage? Bask in the remembrance of the day when you became royalty. If you have not, what is keeping you from answering Jesus's knock today?

Lighthouse at Lake Sumter Landing

Eleven

A Special Purpose

"The flowers appear on the earth; The time of singing is come, And the voice of the turtle-dove is heard in our land" (Song of Solomon 2:12 DARBY)

Wind skims the lake's surface, rippling the water and tousling my hair. I walk the boards past the lighthouse and come to a shaded path where I hear the soft cooing of doves.

I'm intrigued by doves. Their feathers aren't flamboyant or fancy in any respect; they're a subtle earthy color. The song of doves is a quiet, guttural cooing. Doves have a calm, peaceful demeanor.

Although they're common birds, they played a significant role in the Bible. Noah sent out a dove after the flood to see if there was any dry ground. The dove flew around for a while, then flew back to the ark. Noah waited a week and then sent a dove out again. This time it returned with a freshly plucked olive leaf in its beak. Noah knew the water was receding. After another week, Noah sent out a dove a third time. When it didn't return, Noah knew the ground was drying.

The Law required animal sacrifices to atone for the sins of the people. Not all people had herds or flocks, and not all people could afford to purchase animals for their sacrifices. The Lord made accommodations for the poor by accepting the sacrifice of a dove or a pigeon.

When Jesus began his ministry, he asked John to baptize him. As soon as Jesus emerged from the water, the Spirit of God descended upon him in the form of a dove.

The Bible makes more than fifty references to doves, showing us God had a special purpose for these ordinary birds.

Sometimes, we think of ourselves as ordinary. We can't imagine the Lord would have a special purpose for us. The Bible says something different. "But God has chosen the foolish things of the world that he may put to shame the wise; and God has chosen the weak things of the world, that he may put to shame the strong things; and the ignoble things of the world, and the despised, has God chosen" (1 Corinthians 1:27-29, 31 DARBY).

We're not ordinary to God. He paid an extraordinary price to redeem us. We're highly valued by the Lord, and he has a special purpose for us. Our challenge is to discover our purpose and use it to glorify God.

Paul compares the members of the church to the human body. Each member of the human body has a specific purpose and some of the less appealing parts have a greater purpose. In the same way, each member of the church has a specific purpose. No one is unimportant. Some people are blessed with multiple gifts, while others may have one simple gift, but that simple gift has great significance in the kingdom.

Frances was a plain and modest woman who wouldn't catch anyone's attention. She was an ordinary dove who used the gifts she'd been given. She was the first one to greet people as they entered the church. When there was a potluck dinner, she could be found quietly helping in the kitchen. She always helped with VBS, even when she was in her nineties. Frances didn't serve in order to obtain glory. Her humble acts of service were done to honor the Lord. Frances recently went home to be with the Lord, but she is greatly missed. Her gifts enriched the church.

Our gift may be to offer quiet acts of service. Maybe we're a better support person than a leader. We may have the gift of patience or empathy. Maybe we're an encourager. We may prefer working behind the scenes where others don't notice us. No gift is insignificant in the Lord's kingdom. But, his kingdom suffers loss if we undervalue our talents and fail to use them. If God had a special purpose for doves, he surely has great plans for us.

O Lord, may we use our abilities to glorify you.

My child, you are of great value to my kingdom.

A MOMENT OF REFLECTION

Have you discovered your special significance in God's kingdom? What gifts are you using for him?

Atlas Canine Recreation Park

Twelve

We Lift Up Our Souls

"Bring joy to the soul of your servant, for to you, Lord, do I lift up my soul" (Psalm 86:4 WEB).

Two dogs romp across the grass, slowing as they approach each other. After an introductory sniff, the small spotted dog rolls onto its back, exposing its vulnerability and showing deference to the big brown setter.

Dogs exhibit traits of submission or dominance. A submissive dog surrenders itself to a dominant dog by lying down and rolling onto its back. Its posture offers complete control to the dominant dog. In other words, the submissive dog entrusts its life to the dominant dog.

Years ago, we had a golden retriever. Each day after work, my husband play-wrestled with our dog. Inevitably, their playtime ended with our dog submitting itself to my husband.

Cesar Milan, the famous dog behaviorist, teaches dog owners to assert dominant behavior over their pets in order to achieve balance and harmony in the relationship. To avoid chaos in the home, the pet must submit to its master.

A similar struggle occurs in our spiritual relationship. For there to be harmony and balance, we must submit to the Lord in everything. Without proper posturing, we cause chaos in our spiritual lives.

David exhibited a posture of submission to the Lord, and as a result, the Lord said of him, "I have found David the son of Jesse, a man after my own heart, who will do all my will" (Acts 13:22 WEB).

David entrusted himself to the Lord because he knew who God was. "But you, Lord, are a merciful and gracious God, slow to anger, and abundant in loving kindness" (Psalm 86:15 WEB) David willingly submitted to the Lord because he trusted his goodness and faithfulness. He lifted up his soul and trusted the Lord to guard it.

David's confidence came from experience. As a boy shepherd, he trusted the Lord to help him protect the sheep when a lion or bear preyed upon them. The trust David built as a shepherd served as a foundation for the trust he relied upon when he battled the giant Goliath. Remembering how the Lord helped him in the past gave David confidence to trust the Lord in future battles. Each struggle gave David an opportunity to trust God more and more. Each time David trusted the Lord, the strength of his trust increased.

As a brand new Christian, I had no experience with trusting Jesus. I remember praying with trepidation in my heart, not sure the Lord would respond to my prayers. Each prayer was like testing the thickness of ice. My prayers were tentative steps onto a frozen lake that I was not sure would hold my weight. Over time, I learned the Lord's faithfulness was thicker than the ice on a Minnesota lake in winter. Now, I confidently throw myself into the center of the ice because, time and again, the Lord proves his faithfulness. I confidently lift up my soul to the Lord.

We show our trust in God's goodness when we lift up our souls. It is an act of submission, surrendering control to the one who is perfectly dominant. When we lift up our souls, we lie on our backs, exposing our vulnerability to the Lord. We entrust our Heavenly Father with all we hold dear. We trust him with the lives of our loved ones. We surrender to him our finances and our plans. We trust him with our health and safety. When we lift up our souls, we raise our arms toward heaven and say, "It's out of my hands. I trust you, Lord, with my very life." Our Heavenly Father receives our surrender as a precious gift of faith. It shows our trust in his goodness.

O Lord, we entrust you with our deepest need. To you, we lift up our souls.

You can trust me with every vulnerable part of you. I am your faithful Father, and you are my precious child.

A MOMENT OF REFLECTION

Are you willing to lift up your soul to the Lord? Write down an area of your life that you haven't surrendered. Now step onto the ice and test the Lord's goodness. He will not disappoint you.

Burnsed Recreation Center

Thirteen

Knowing the Hope

"The eyes of your understanding being enlightened; that ye may know what is the hope of his calling" (Ephesians 1:18 KJV).

Purple grasses sway and dip to a tune only they hear. Birds swoop down from palm trees and strut across the ground. Irises, as if competing in a beauty pageant, hold their heads high and unfold their lovely white skirts to show off the gold and purple embroidery.

I notice these woodland wonders while I leisurely rock on the porch of Burnsed Recreation Center. There are glorious gifts of nature all around me, but too often I overlook them. The Creator teaches me about himself through the wonders of creation. When I rush through my days, I miss his lessons. The Lord wants me to slow down and notice his Presence all around me so I can know the hope to which he's called me.

The Apostle Paul went to the city of Ephesus to share the hope of God with the people of that city. Ephesus was located in what is now modern-day Turkey. During Paul's time, Ephesus was a great port city known as The Light of Asia. It was known for the great Temple of Artemis, also called the Temple of Diana. It was considered one of the Seven Wonders of the World. People made a living selling idols of Diana. Paul went to the city to preach about the one true God. Although he faced great opposition, many Ephesians believed the truth Paul taught and their hearts were enlightened.

For several years, Paul preached the gospel to the Ephesians. Because of his work in Ephesus, "all that inhabited Asia heard the word of the Lord, both Jews and Greeks" (Acts 19:10 DARBY). Those who opened their hearts came to know the hope that their lifeless idols couldn't provide. Paul spoke of the true and living God who saves mankind from their sins.

On the day of Pentecost, the Apostle Peter shared the hope with a crowd in Jerusalem. God-fearing Jews from every nation gathered to celebrate the holiday. Peter spoke to the crowd, telling the listeners God promised to pour out his Spirit on all people. His salvation would no longer be only for the Jews. Peter said that in the last days "whoever will call on the name of the Lord will be saved" (Acts 2:21 WEB). Jews and Gentiles alike would know the hope of salvation and the hope of spending eternity in heaven.

Both Peter and Paul spread the truth of the gospel so people everywhere could know the hope we have in Jesus Christ.

Our God is not a lifeless marble idol like Diana of the Ephesians. Paul said the One who created heaven and earth doesn't live in man-made temples. He is near to each of us. In fact, we live and move in him. Our God is alive and wants us to know the hope he offers to us, a hope that washes away sins, a hope that promises eternal life.

We can know the hope, and we can know the One who is our hope. We come to know someone by spending time with him. Our Lord, the God of Heaven, wants us to spend time with him. He has wisdom to impart to us. He wants to guide us along the right path. This can't happen if we hurry through each day. We come to know our Heavenly Father by spending time in his presence, by talking with him and sitting at his feet to learn from him. We come to know his touch when we crawl into his arms to pray. Our God breathes life into our weary spirits and gives us unfailing hope.

Dear Lord, please forgive us for rushing through our days without noticing you. Help us to slow down and savor the wonder of who you are.

Precious child, I have so much to share with you. Take my hand and stroll with me.

A MOMENT OF REFLECTION

Look around you. In what way is God revealing himself to you? Be still and contemplate the one who is your hope.

The Villages Polo Club

Fourteen

Where Is Your Trust?

"Some trust in chariots and some in horses, but we will remember the name of the Lord our God" (Psalm 20:7 KJV).

Looking across acres of grassy polo fields, I imagine horses with muscles quivering, awesome beasts endowed with strength and speed. In frenzied excitement, they charge into the fray of a polo match.

"He paws in the valley and rejoices in his strength. He goes out to meet the armed men. He eats up the ground with fierceness and rage, neither does he stand still at the sound of the trumpet" (Job 39:21, 24 WEB). It's no wonder an army equipped with horses and chariots sparked fear in the people being attacked. Sennacherib, the king of Assyria, had a powerful army of soldiers, horsemen, and chariots. He had been invading nations and seizing their land. He sent a bold threat to Hezekiah, king of Judah, telling him he may as well surrender because Jehovah couldn't protect him from the Assyrian army.

With great fear in his heart, Hezekiah prayed for deliverance. The Lord sent a message through Isaiah the prophet. "Be not afraid of the words which thou hast heard" (2 Kings 19:6 KJV).

The Lord intervened by causing Sennacherib to be summoned home so he couldn't attack Hezekiah. After a while, Sennacherib taunted Hezekiah again, sending a threatening letter. Hezekiah went to the temple and spread out the letter before the Lord. He prayed, "And now, Jehovah our God, I beseech thee, save us out of his hand, that all kingdoms of the earth may know that thou, Jehovah, art God, thou only" (2 Kings 19:19 DARBY).

During the night, the Lord fought the battle for Hezekiah by striking down 185,000 men. The rest of the soldiers withdrew. A while later, Sennacherib was struck down and killed by two of his sons.

We serve a mighty God. We serve the God who created horses and gave them their strength and speed. We serve the God who causes nations to crumble under his mighty hand. Horses and chariots, soldiers and kings, have only the power given them by the Lord.

The same is true of circumstances that threaten us. They may seem as powerful as an army of horses and chariots, but the Lord is more powerful than any circumstance.

In her book, *The Hiding Place*, Corrie ten Boom writes about her experiences in a Nazi concentration camp. She was assigned to one of the worst women's barracks. It was flea-infested. Each night as she tried to sleep, she was tormented by fleas. She couldn't understand why the Lord made her endure such horrid conditions. One day, she realized the fleas were God's protection. The women in her dormitory didn't suffer abusive attacks from the soldiers at night because the soldiers wouldn't go into the flea-infested barracks. The Lord used fleas to protect Corrie from something much worse. During the rest of her imprisonment, the Lord continued to show his power in unusual ways.

At times, we're confronted with situations that fill us with anxiety. We don't understand why the Lord allows them, and our faith is shaken. Like nations quaking before an army of horses and chariots, we quake in the face of unstable finances. We cower when confronted with a bad medical diagnosis. Family problems fill us with anxiety, but we don't need to fear. We have examples of people who trusted a faithful God. Hezekiah placed his fears before the Lord, then waited for the Lord to act on his behalf. Corrie ten Boom found that God's plan, though unpleasant, saved her from a much worse fate. We hear stories in the Bible and in everyday life that proclaim God's faithfulness. When our hearts tremble, we can confidently go to the Lord for help. He'll show us his power over our circumstances. Nothing compares to his mighty strength. The Lord is worthy of our trust.

May we always trust in the name of the Lord our God.

Precious one, call upon me, and I will help you.

In what ways are you willing to trust the Lord with your greatest fears? Write a prayer asking for his help.

Glenview Country Club Entrance

Fifteen

The Lord Is Good

"Give thanks to Yahweh, for he is good...

He turns a desert into a pool of water, and a dry land into water" (Psalm 107:1, 35 WEB).

A series of tiered pools graces the entrance to Glenview Country Club. As water trickles from pool to pool, it flows over rocks and under stone archways. White ibis flock along the edges of the water, feasting on the abundant food the pools provide. Flowers adorn the lush area.

As I walk beside the flowing pools of water, I think of the stories woven through Psalm 107. The psalmist recalls how the Lord turned the desert into pools as he continually helped Israel during times of trouble. The Lord was good to them whenever they called out to him. Each story concludes with the words, "Give thanks to the Lord, for he is good; his love endures forever" (Psalm 107:1 NIV).

When Israel wandered in a desert land, they were hungry and thirsty. They called out to the Lord. He heard their cry and led them to a place where they would have food to eat and water to drink. Instead of dry pools, he gave them springs of water. The Lord was good to them.

I lived part of my life by dry pools. I was hungry and thirsty, but I relied upon myself to satisfy my needs. My vision was horizontal rather than vertical. The dry pools the world offered couldn't quench my thirst. When I finally called out to the Lord, he heard my cry and satisfied my thirsty soul. The Lord is good.

The psalmist tells the story of people who sat in darkness and deepest gloom because they had rebelled against the Lord. When they called out to him with repentant hearts, he saved them.

Things happen in life that knock us down. We may find ourselves stuck in the boggy muck at the bottom of the pool. The more we cling to the muck, the deeper we sink. It could be that, like the Israelites, we despise the counsel of the Lord and follow our own desires, partaking in activities that leave us lying in the muck. It could be that a tragedy causes us to feel so hopeless that we let our thoughts sink until our mind gets stuck in the deepest gloom. At that point, only the Lord can free us from the suction. If we call out to him, he'll lift us out of the bog and put us back on firm ground.

A friend of mine suffered with an addiction from trying to soothe a deep emotional hurt. The more she tried to soothe herself, the deeper she sank into the muck. When she finally called upon the Lord for help, he freed her from her addiction. For the first time, after all her years of trying, her pain was healed. The Lord is good.

The Lord never leaves us or forsakes us; we are the ones who turn from him. We may not realize we're standing with our backs to the Lord until we suffer the consequences of ignoring him. If our lives seem dry and we hunger and thirst for something more, we can ask ourselves if we've reserved a place for the Lord in our lives. Do we read his word to gain wisdom? Do we pray for help and guidance? Do we remember his many blessings of the past?

If we answer no, our stories may be similar to the Israelites' stories in Psalm 107. They only found relief from their troubles when they called upon the Lord. Just as the Lord saved them, he'll also help us if we call out to him. He'll place us near sparkling pools of pure water. He'll quench our thirst so we'll never thirst again. The Lord offers the same soul-quenching water to all who call upon him because he is good and his love lasts forever.

O Lord, we desperately need you. Help us.

Precious one, my love endures forever. I will help you.

A MOMENT OF REFLECTION

Read Psalm 107. How do you identify with any of the people? Write about it.

Magnolia Blossoms

Sixteen

Victory Brings Peace

"These things have I spoken to you that in me ye might have peace. In the world ye have tribulation; but be of good courage: I have overcome the world" (John 16:33 DARBY).

Southern magnolia trees flank the corners of the porch like sentries guarding their posts. The branches reach out to visitors with peace offerings of creamy, sweet-scented flowers.

From the porch of Eisenhower Recreation Center, I enjoy the beauty of the grand white blooms. They're a symbol of peace, reminding me of the military victories that have allowed me to live in peace. The United States has experienced decades of peace thanks to the victories our soldiers won on foreign shores. Other nations fear the strength of our military. As a result, we live in peace.

Jesus wanted us to live in peace, but he knew that wasn't possible without a hard-fought victory. He fought the battle that brought peace to his followers. The battle took place on earth, but it had a far-reaching impact in the spiritual realm.

The crucifixion of Christ was that bloody battle. His resurrection was the victory that brought peace for all believers. No longer could our spiritual enemy hold the threat of death over our heads. Jesus' victory brought us peace with God. For Christians, death is not a threat; it's a reward. The Apostle Paul expressed it this way, "For me to live [is] Christ, and to die gain" (Philippians 1:21 DARBY).

The enemy, Satan, knows he's lost the war; but while he has time on earth, he torments and harasses us. That's why Jesus told his disciples they would have trouble in this world.

Ephesians 6 admonishes us to put on the armor of God so we can stand against the enemy's schemes. The belt of truth is the Bible, which helps us to distinguish truth from lies. The breastplate of righteousness is a gift we receive when the Lord purifies us from our sins. While we wear our breastplate, the enemy can't declare us unrighteous before the judgment seat of God Almighty.

The shield of faith protects us from the flaming darts of our enemy. He throws darts of doubt, fear, and temptation at us all day long. If we let down our shields, we'll be struck by one of his darts. The helmet of salvation protects our minds from the enemy's message of doom. When we're saved, we don't need to doubt our final destination. Our eternal condition is secure because our name is written in the Lamb's Book of Life.

Our one offensive weapon is the sword of the Spirit. Jesus showed us how to use it when he responded to the devil in the wilderness. The Lord answered each temptation with Scripture. It's vital that we keep our swords sharpened by studying God's word so when temptations sneak up on us, we have a weapon that can strike them down.

Finally, we're instructed to wear the gospel of peace on our feet. The Lord wants us to carry the good news of his victory to others so they can enjoy the blessing of peace.

On earth, we'll have conflict. We'll battle against our fleshly weaknesses, and we'll wrestle with the problems life throws our way. However, these are merely scuffles to distract us from the peace Jesus won for us. Our armor helps us withstand the continual testing of our faith. The enemy knows he's lost the war, so he tries to cause us misery in each skirmish. His assaults are ineffective because we're already champions through the victory Jesus won.

The peace Jesus won is for all. The door stands open for anyone who wants to enter and partake of the sweet victory over death. The Lord is not willing that any should perish. His hard-fought peace is for all who will receive it.

Like the magnolia trees holding out flowers of peace, Jesus holds out his nail-scarred hands as symbols of the victory that bought our eternal peace.

O Lord, we thank you for the sweet gift of peace.

Child, I won the victory for you.

A MOMENT OF REFLECTION

Are you experiencing the peace Jesus won for you? If not, why? What is obstructing your attainment of it?

Live Oaks Park

Seventeen

Favored by God

"For thou, Jehovah, wilt bless the righteous [man]; with favour wilt thou surround him as [with] a shield" (Psalm 5:12 DARBY).

A secluded path winds through a small park near the Haciendas of Mission Hills. I enter an enchanted forest where Spanish moss drapes like gauzy shawls from the branches of live oak trees. Surrounded by the silvery fibers of nature's swaying veils, I feel encased in God's love and I think of how the Lord surrounds me with his favor.

Favor is an act of gracious kindness. God showers us with kindness even before we know him. I grew up unchurched, knowing little about spiritual matters. I walked some paths that led to ungodly pursuits. The Lord was merciful and spared me from many consequences that could have occurred because of my poor choices. His love guided me toward a good path.

Through a series of coincidences, the Lord led me to a church that nurtured me with spiritual love and biblical truth. I was like a dry sponge absorbing every drop of information. My faith grew along with my understanding of the Bible. The spiritual foundation I acquired equipped me for the future plans God had for me. His favor surrounded me as I matured in my Christian walk.

I learned that sometimes God's favor doesn't happen the way we expect it to. Sometimes it is hidden in disappointment. I discovered this after preparing for a new position in my job. For two years, I taught a third grade class all day. Several nights a week, I took courses at a university. I studied to acquire the advanced degree I needed for a new position in my school district. Many co-workers assured me the position would be an open door, but the door slammed in my face. I expected God to intervene on my behalf, but he didn't. When I learned someone outside of the district had been hired for the position I wanted, I was heartbroken. I couldn't understand why I didn't get the job I had set my heart on. I went home to my bedroom, sat with my back against my bed, and stared blankly ahead of me. Where was God's favor?

Sad and hurt, I applied for a similar position elsewhere. When I was hired, I was paired with an Asian coworker who worshipped Buddha. She had heard the gospel and asked me many questions about Christianity. As our friendship grew, her questions increased. We spent a lot of time discussing the Bible. I shared passages of Scripture with her, and I answered her questions with the truth I had been taught. Eventually, she responded to the Lord's call upon her heart and became a Christian. She evangelized her family, who also became believers. During a visit to her country of origin, she shared the gospel with all who would listen. Because of her, the gospel spread among people who didn't know Jesus.

The Lord's plans to place me in that job were much better than my plans of changing to a new position in my old district. Because of God's favor, my bad experience evolved into a wonderful blessing for me and others.

Our Heavenly Father delights in blessing his children. At times, his favor may be disguised within challenges or disappointments. We may have to pass through difficulties before we see the good plans God has for us. No matter how bad our struggle may be, we can be confident of this: God does not disappoint. When we love the Lord, he works in all of our circumstances for good. The Lord's plans may differ from ours, and we may have to wait to see the blessings, but we will see them. God's favor always surrounds his children.

Heavenly Father, we rejoice as you wrap us with your favor.

Precious one, you can trust me completely. I will never disappoint you.

A MOMENT OF REFLECTION

Can you identify circumstances that you attribute to God's favor working in your life? What incidents seemed like struggles at the time but turned out to be blessings?

Gazebo at Sumter Landing

Eighteen

A Shelter in the Storm

"He will cover you with his feathers. Under his wings you will take refuge" (Psalm 91:4 WEB).

Wind whipped up waves on the lake. Rain tap-danced on the tin roof of the gazebo and polka dotted the water with ringlets. In the tiny pavilion, I took shelter from the sudden storm.

I recalled times when the Lord sheltered me during storms in my life. I ran to him through pelting rain as he called to me, "Hurry to your place of shelter, far from the tempest and storm." My heart calmed at the sound of his voice. As I nestled beneath his soft wings, the Lord dried the raindrops from my face.

The Lord sheltered Noah through the worst storm in the history of the earth—The Flood. Because of man's extreme wickedness, the Lord was grieved and decided to wipe out mankind, but Noah found favor in God's eyes. The Lord told Noah to build an ark. Noah obeyed the Lord and constructed a huge boat that would hold his family, plus a male and female of each type of animal.

At the appointed time, Noah and his wife, his three sons, and their wives entered the ark filled with animals. God closed the door and sealed it. Then, a storm assaulted the earth for forty days until the waters rose twenty feet above the mountains. Every living thing on earth was destroyed, but the Lord protected Noah in the ark.

When the floodwaters receded enough for Noah to step onto dry ground, he built an altar to the Lord and sacrificed burnt offerings on it. The Lord was pleased and made a covenant never again to destroy all living creatures on earth. The Lord blessed Noah and his sons and told them to be fruitful and multiply. Then the Lord said, "I set my rainbow in the cloud, and it will be a sign of a covenant between me and the earth" (Genesis 9:13 WEB).

Storms occur today, not to the extent of The Flood, but they still cause damage and loss of life. I remember when Hurricane Sandy slammed the east coast. People boarded up their homes and retreated inland to safety. Once the storm fizzled out, people returned to view the wreckage it left behind. It took years for communities in New York and New Jersey to recover from the tremendous damage that one storm caused.

Physical storms remind us of the incredible force of nature and man's vulnerability. But there are other types of storms that strike us. These are storms that whirl into our lives causing destruction in places where we're most vulnerable. These storms may attack the well-being of our families. They may be storms that destroy sacred relationships. Some storms blow through our bodies causing critical health issues. These are the storms of life, and their damage can be more intense than that of physical storms. They affect our minds and our hearts. They fill us with such anxiety we don't know where to take shelter.

When these storms come, the Lord sees the circumstances that rage against us. He calls to us through the rain, reminding us that he is our place of shelter. He invites us to curl up in his lap until the storm passes. When we're encircled by his powerful arms, our tension relaxes because we find a safe haven. The One who has power to destroy the earth with a physical storm also has power to calm the storms of life.

God is our refuge as long as we run to him. If we choose to stand in the pelting rain, we won't experience his sheltering presence. If we decide to brave the storms in our own strength, we miss the comfort of his soft resting place. Our Heavenly Father wants to cover us. He waits with outstretched arms for us to run to him.

O Lord, when storms assail us, we want to hide beneath your mighty wings.

Little one, hurry to me. I'm your shelter in the storm.

A MOMENT OF REFLECTION

When has the Lord been your shelter in the storm? Write a prayer thanking God for his care.

Sunrise

Nineteen

A New Day

"Forgetting the things which are behind and stretching forward to the things which are before, I press on toward the goal for the prize of the high calling of God in Christ Jesus" (Philippians 3:13-14 WEB).

Psychedelic colors, wild brush strokes of purple and orange, splash the dark sky. Gradually, brilliant light washes away the colors and there is no trace of darkness. Night is forgotten in the radiant dawning of a new day.

With a grand celebration of light, sunrise signals the beginning of a new day. It ushers in hope, endless possibilities, and change. Yesterday disappears with the night, and we get a blank sheet of paper on which we can paint any picture we want.

The Apostle Paul was given such an opportunity. Originally known as Saul of Tarsus, he was a devout Pharisee who thought he was defending God's ways by persecuting the new sect of Christian believers. He was convinced his actions were right and pleasing to God.

"But Saul still breathing threats and slaughter against the disciples of the Lord came to the high priest, and asked for letters from him to the synagogues of Damascus" (Acts 9:1-2 WEB). Paul wanted legal authority to arrest followers of Christ.

Haven't we acted like Saul, doing things we thought were right at the time, but later realizing they were wrong? Memories of those acts become blots in our past, dark areas that haunt our spirits and cause us to struggle beneath a load of guilt. Or maybe we limp along, maimed by wrong acts committed against us. We haul heavy bags filled with bitterness and resentment over the injustices we suffered. Rehashing our memories keeps us trapped in the night.

As Saul thundered down the road toward Damascus, a bright light flashed around him and he fell to the ground. Jesus spoke from heaven, "Saul, Saul, why do you persecute me?" (Acts 9:4 NIV). Saul was blinded and told to wait in the city for instructions. A man named Ananias went to Saul and said, "Brother Saul, the Lord, who appeared to you on the road by which you came, has sent me, that you may receive your sight and be filled with the Holy Spirit" (Acts 9:17 WEB). When Ananias touched Saul's eyes, his sight was restored and he got up and was baptized. Saul began to preach the good news of Jesus in the synagogues. Because Saul turned from his wrong ways, the Lord forgave him and gave him a chance to start over.

When the light of understanding opens our eyes to see our mistakes, we have a choice to make. We can hold onto the past, allowing pain or regret to drag us down; or we can accept the gift of a new day and begin to think differently. The Lord will wash away our guilt. He'll free us from the shackles of resentment. God's forgiveness will lift us up.

The blood of Jesus washes away our sins just as the sun washes away the night. The love of the Lord soothes our pain like a healing balm that restores us to health. Our guilt, hurt and sadness fade away with the night sky. Experiencing the Lord's forgiveness and healing is like opening our front doors at sunrise and stepping into a sparkling new day.

Our Heavenly Father wants us to begin each day with untainted thoughts, turning away from pasts we can't change. With each sunrise, he beckons us to reach out and embrace a day filled with hope and promise, to rejoice in the possibilities he places before us. The rising sun is a reminder that God gives us a new chance, a new start, a new day. The Lord's amazing gift of newness allows us to forget what lies behind us and to press on toward the life to which we've been called.

Lord Jesus, please forgive us for the wrongs of yesterday.

Precious child, you are cleansed. Come into the sunlight of a new day.

A MOMENT OF REFLECTION

How are you stuck in the night because of guilt, bitterness, or resentment? Why not release them to the Lord and step into the light of a new day? List two things weighing you down. Surrender them to the Lord in prayer this day.

Brownwood Paddock Square

Twenty

Stars Over the Square

"Lift your eyes on high and see! Who hath created these things, bringing out their host by number?" (Isaiah 40:26 DARBY).

The sky was a deep blue canvas. The Master Artist painted the moon a silver slash. He dangled stars like diamond pendants from its slender curve.

Last night, amidst the music in Brownwood Paddock Square, I looked up. All sounds faded into white noise. I was awed by the night sky, realizing a star-filled canopy spread over the entire earth. I felt infinitesimal in the presence of an immense universe. The Creator dazzled me with his magnificent work.

In the thirty-eighth chapter of Job we read about the work the Lord did in the heavens. He created the constellations that appear during certain seasons. He determined the laws that govern the skies so that morning arrives according to his plan. We learn that while the Lord was setting the earth's foundations, the morning stars sang. Scientists confirm that stars emit radio waves which make a high-pitched sound when recorded on earth. Stars actually sing.

Not only does God determine the number of stars, of which scientists approximate there are 100 octillion, he also calls each one by name. "He calleth them all by name; through the greatness of his might and strength of power, not one faileth" (Isaiah 40:26 DARBY).

We have a God who is able to keep track of stars more numerous than any number I've ever heard of. He gives each star a name and watches over each one. If he can do that, he can certainly keep track of all that happens in the lives of those he created in his own image. The God who watches over us exhibits his greatness in the stars.

If we were to zoom in for a closer look at the stars, we'd see that most of them are bigger than our sun. They emit a rainbow of colors, but the colors blend together as the light travels to earth, so to our eyes, stars appear to be white. Cooler stars are really red, and the hottest stars are actually blue. What we perceive to be twinkling doesn't originate with the stars. It happens as light rays bounce through the various densities of the earth's atmosphere. This makes the light appear to twinkle.

The study of the heavens is fascinating. With each piece of information I learn, the more I'm impressed with the Designer. Even though I'm astounded by God's works, sometimes I find myself doubting his power in my day-to-day life. I question whether he really sees my struggles. I wonder if he will help me. My faith wavers. I wish I would be more steadfast, but sometimes I allow fear to control my mind. Even the disciples, who were present for all of Jesus' miracles, doubted his power.

One evening, after a long day of ministering to the crowds, Jesus asked the disciples to take him in a boat to the other side of the lake where he could rest. As the boat crossed the water, a storm broke out. Waves nearly swamped the boat. In a panic, the disciples woke Jesus from a sound sleep, hollering that they were going to drown. Jesus got up and rebuked the winds and the waves. Everything became calm. The disciples looked at each other, astonished at yet another miracle. Then Jesus said, "Why are you so afraid? How is it that you have no faith?" (Mark 4:40 WEB).

The God of the universe asks us to trust him. He asks us to place our anxieties into his mighty hands, hands that formed the heavens and earth. He asks us to trust him with the outcome. Our Heavenly Father uses the stars to remind us of his awesome power. Nothing is too hard for the Creator of the universe. The One who calls each star by name knows our names.

O Lord, Creator of the heavens, help our unbelief.

My child, don't be afraid to believe in me. My plans are perfect.

A MOMENT OF REFLECTION

What do the stars say to you about our mighty God? How do they confirm his power?

Beams of Light

Twenty-One

Children of Light

"For you were once darkness, but are now light in the Lord. Walk as children of light" (Ephesians 5:8 WEB).

The big sky over Sweetgum Golf Course was shrouded in thick cloud cover. The air hung heavy and dismal. Suddenly, golden shafts of light pierced through the clouds, and iridescent beams of sunlight transformed the sky from gray to gold.

Before I knew the Lord, my mind felt like it was shrouded in heavy cloud cover. I lived the way I thought I should, charting my own course but not realizing I was drifting aimlessly.

A ship captain who navigates by the stars lacks a clear point of reference when the sky is heavy with clouds. His ship drifts in whatever direction the wind and waves carry it. Once the clouds lift, the captain can plot a clear course.

Until the Lord's light pierced my darkness, I was like a drifting ship without a clear course. I didn't realize there was a better way to live until the Creator of light illuminated my way. The Lord charted a path for me so I didn't have to meander beneath the clouds. His chart pointed me to a heavenly destination.

When I was living in darkness, I was spiritually blind. I didn't understand that life held a deeper purpose and that God had plans for me. Once the Lord broke through my darkness, I saw things from a spiritual perspective. I felt like blinders had been taken from my eyes, blinders I never knew I was wearing. My muddled thoughts cleared, and life made sense to me.

Jesus said, "The lamp of the body is the eye. Therefore when your eye is good, your whole body is also full of light; but when it is evil, your body also is full of darkness" (Luke 11:34 WEB). People who live in spiritual darkness stumble into all kinds of trouble because they can't see the Lord's path. They lack the spiritual insight that comes from the Lord. Only those who carry his light within can see the path. The Lord wants us to be sensitive and compassionate to those who can't see the way.

There's an activity to sensitize workers to the visual challenges some of their customers may have. Workers wear glasses smeared with Vaseline while they try to go about their duties. By the end of the activity, the workers develop patience and compassion for their customers who are sight-challenged.

As Christians we need to have compassion toward those who are spiritually impaired. We need to remember how we also stumbled in darkness before we found the light.

In the Apostle Paul's letter to the Ephesians, he reminds the believers they used to walk in darkness, indulging in the deeds of darkness. After learning the truth, they became children of light. With that privilege comes responsibility. Paul encouraged the new believers to develop new values consistent with the Lord's teachings. He admonished them to practice good, righteous and truthful deeds in order to please the Lord.

In a parable, Jesus tells us what pleases the Lord. He says no one hides a light beneath a bowl, rather they put it on a lampstand to lighten the room for all (Matthew 5:15).

When we become children of light, we have a responsibility to share our light with the rest of the world. The Lord wants us to shine into the surrounding world to light the way for those who stumble beneath the clouds.

God's light changes us. It transforms our minds and hearts. Where once we were blinded by darkness, we're enlightened by truth. The Lord wants his qualities of goodness, righteousness, and truth to radiate through us to others. He wants us to shimmer in the darkness to lead others to his light. When the Lord puts his light in us, he wants us to shine for him.

Lord, help us imitate you so we radiate your light to others.

Little one, my light is meant to be shared.

A MOMENT OF REFLECTION

Are you walking beneath the clouds? Ask the Lord to shine his light upon you. Are you a child of light? Ask the Lord to help you shine in the darkness.

Savannah Center Patio

Twenty-Two

A Perfect Husband

"For thy Maker is thy husband; Jehovah of hosts is his name" (Isaiah 54:5 ASV).

Dainty white petals flutter from crepe myrtle trees and sprinkle the brick patio. As if preparing for a wedding, white lattice tea tables stand ready for guests. I feel like a bride as I walk into this lacy setting on the Savannah Center patio.

Our daughter Christine recently got married. Prior to her wedding, she was in the Peace Corps living in the country of Ghana on the continent of Africa. She was far from home and living in a very foreign culture. As it turned out, she fell in love with a young Ghanaian man. She brought him home to meet her family, during which time he asked for her hand in marriage. My husband asked him about the custom in Ghana when a man proposes to a girl. He said the groom gives the family a goat as a bride-price. My husband declined the goat, but Christine and Paa Kwesi combined a little bit of each culture in their wedding ceremony. In a prayer, my husband asked the Lord to bless their marriage.

Women remember their wedding day and all the days leading up to it, days filled with every possible emotion. After the wedding, a woman becomes a wife and her marriage begins. Her life now includes a husband. It doesn't take long for her to realize he isn't perfect, but neither is she. Because of their imperfections, their marriage goes through rocky patches.

Sometimes a marriage doesn't end well. The Lord understands the fear and shame a rejected woman feels. He compares it to the way Israel felt when God rejected them. But God's rejection was temporary. In Isaiah 54 we read that the Lord called them back. This passage shows us the depth of God's love for his chosen bride Israel. He is a compassionate and forgiving husband. The Lord is a perfect husband.

In Ephesians 5, Jesus calls upon husbands to follow his example of pure love. He loved the church, his bride, so much that he gave himself up for her. His goal was to make her holy and radiant. She would be like a flawless diamond.

In our culture, it's customary for a young man to purchase a diamond for the girl he hopes to marry. A diamond is a highly prized gem. A man presents it to the woman he considers to be his gem. In a way, a diamond is an American bride-price.

The sacrifice of Jesus Christ was the bride-price God paid for us. God the Father offered the life of his Son in order to purchase us as his bride. Our bride-price was paid with blood.

Whether we're single, married, or widowed, the Lord is our perfect match. No earthly man or woman compares to Jesus. He is our true soulmate. We can't truly grasp how wide and long and high and deep his love is. Jesus paid the bride-price for us when we were worthless. He loved us when we were dirty from our long trek through sin. He desired us when we were undesirable.

Imagine being dressed in rags and covered in grime, plodding along, lost with no destination in sight. Then, in the distance, you see dust rising on the trail in front of you. It's a man on a horse. As he gets closer, you notice he's dressed in pure white. He locks eyes with you as he approaches. He stops his horse and descends from the saddle. He takes your filthy hand in his clean hand and bends down on one knee. With eyes overflowing with love, he speaks. He says he's been following you for a long time. You are priceless to him, and he values you more than his own life. He asks you to be his wife.

The man is Jesus. We are the woman. If we accept his proposal, he asks one thing of us---to have first place in our hearts. Jesus wants us to always gaze upon him with the sparkling eyes of a bride. He promises to love and cherish us forever.

Precious Lord, we give ourselves to you.

My darling, my dove, love me with all of your heart, soul, strength, and mind.

A MOMENT OF REFLECTION

Have you accepted Jesus' proposal? Have you given him first place in your heart? It's not too late. Write a prayer to the Lord.

Morse Boulevard Recreation Trail

Twenty-Three

A Moment to Treasure

"My beloved spoke, and said to me, 'Rise up, my love, my beautiful one, and come away'" (Song of Solomon 2:10 WEB).

Sun drapes my shoulders with warm silk. A gentle breeze plays with my hair as wisps of clouds drift lazily across a dazzling blue sky. In this perfect moment, my senses tingle with delight.

This lovely day is a gift from God. His goodness overwhelms me while I walk along the recreation trail. I feel his soft touch on my cheek, and I hear him saying, "Come away with me, my beautiful one." I lift my face heavenward and smile. This is a moment to treasure.

Song of Solomon records an exchange between two lovers who are overwhelmed by their love for one another. They compare each other's beauty to nature: a rose of Sharon, a lily of the valley, an apple tree filled with sweet fruit. Their adulations express their passion as they create moments they will always treasure in their hearts.

In the seventh chapter of Luke, we read of a woman who was moved by her passion for the Savior. The woman, well known for her sinful life, heard that Jesus was nearby and she entered the house where Jesus was dining. As he reclined at the table, the woman crouched at his feet weeping. She washed his feet with her tears and dried them with her hair. She continuously kissed his feet through her tears. She then poured expensive perfume over them. The woman went to Jesus humbled by shame and regret. He sent her away forgiven. The love and forgiveness of Jesus created a moment the woman would always treasure.

My friend Evi went through a very sad time. She found comfort by the ocean where she could be alone with the Lord.

Sitting on a secluded beach with tears sliding down her cheeks, she would pray, read Scripture, and sing hymns. No matter how difficult her problems, Evi would seek comfort in the Lord. He would revive her spirit so she could return home refreshed. Still, after a few days, the sadness of her problems would creep back in.

One particular weekend, Evi drove to the beach to be with the Lord in her special place. Once again she asked the Lord to refresh her weary spirit, but she was so overcome by sadness she just stared numbly ahead of her. Suddenly, something in the surf caught her attention. When she sat up to look more intently, she saw a school of dolphins diving and splashing in the water directly in front of her. Dolphins were one of her favorite creatures. Their unexpected appearance at that particular time was a gift from the Lord. It brought immense joy to her heart. In her time of need, the God of Hope gave her a gift designed just for her. It was a moment she'll always treasure.

The Lord designs special moments for us to cherish. He creates an abundance of gifts in nature—sparkling skies, smiling flowers, gentle breezes. Some of these gifts are intended just for us because our Creator knows us intimately and he knows what brings joy to our hearts. The Lord places these special treasures along our way. The sweet melody of birds and the brilliant colors of a sunrise are gifts of romance from our Heavenly Father. He wants his gifts to ignite our passion for him. He wants us to respond to him with intense emotion. He's thrilled when we become dizzy in his presence, when we open our arms and twirl with joy. Our holy ardor delights him.

The lover of our souls romances us with gifts and special moments to treasure. He awes us through nature. The next time we're thrilled by a natural wonder, we can look heavenward and smile. The Lord is charming our spirits because his love for us is fervent. When he beckons to us, let's run to his arms and fall into his embrace.

O Lord, our hearts burn with passion for you.

My darling, my beautiful one, come and dance with me.

A MOMENT OF REFLECTION

Today, look for the gifts the Lord placed along your path. Write about the special moments you treasure.

Open Houses in The Villages

Twenty-Four

Welcome Home

"In my father's house are many homes. If it weren't so, I would have told you. I am going to prepare a place for you" (John 14:2 WEB).

My husband and I flew to The Villages to find our dream home. We visited house after house. I had a headache from the stress of trying to choose one before flying back to New Jersey to sell our other house. After two days of looking, our realtor drove us to the next house on our list. The moment I opened the door, the house breathed, "Welcome home!" Its walls wrapped around me like a comfy shirt. My husband and I smiled at each other. Turning to the realtor we said, "This is the one."

As much as I love my new house, I know it's only a temporary home. My true home is in heaven. Earth is the place I live while waiting to arrive at my eternal dwelling place. Since this world isn't my permanent home, I don't want strong attachments to the things this world offers.

Recently, I visited my sister in her home state. I saw many of the sights and visited many famous landmarks. Her state was a beautiful place to visit, but I didn't make permanent plans while I was there. I didn't look for a job or consider buying a house. I knew I was leaving at the end of the week. As much as I enjoyed my visit, I knew my home was back in Florida.

In the twelfth chapter of Hebrews, the author commends people who live their earthly lives with a heavenly focus. They consider themselves aliens and strangers on earth. They live with a focus on their eternal home in heaven.

Jesus admonishes us not to store up treasures on earth. Eventually, they'll disintegrate and we'll have nothing. The only treasures that last are heavenly treasures.

In Matthew 19, Jesus tells the story of a rich young man who claimed he had kept all the commandments since his youth. Wanting to secure a place in heaven, the young man asked Jesus what he should do. Jesus told him to sell his possessions and give his money to the poor. When the man heard that, he walked away sad. His heart was captured by his possessions.

Unlike the rich young man, we may not treasure possessions, but we may treasure other things – time, talents, or family. If we value them above the Lord, they've captured our hearts. Anything that captures our hearts distracts us from God and we forget this world isn't our true home. Our priorities change. Instead of living to please the Lord, we live to acquire, retain, and guard our treasures.

My husband and I own a seasonal rental cottage. Let's imagine we have renters who stay in our cottage for three months. During that time, they replace the windows, enlarge the deck, and enclose the porch. They put down new floors and new carpeting. They repaint the interior and exterior. At the end of three months, they leave. Their investment was foolish because they didn't invest in their permanent home. In the same way, we want our greatest investment to be in our heavenly home. We don't want the Lord to look upon us as foolish renters.

The Lord provides for us while we live on earth. He provides houses for us to live in because he knows we need shelter. But one day, everything we own will disappear. If we allow the transient things of earth to claim our hearts, our priorities are misplaced. We'll end up with a treasure trove of worthless items. By evaluating how we use our money, time, and energy we can determine if we're pleasing the Lord.

When we use our possessions, talents, or expertise to bring glory to God, he becomes our priority and we begin to store up heavenly treasures. Then, when our time on earth is over, we won't regret leaving anything behind. We'll be thrilled to arrive at our eternal home.

Father, we eagerly look forward to living in the place you prepared for us.

On that day you'll hear, "Welcome home, precious child!"

A MOMENT OF REFLECTION

How can you refocus your energies to create heavenly treasures?

Lake Sumter Landing Market Square

Twenty-Five

Shining Through the Rain

"Yahweh, let the light of your face shine on us" (Psalm 4:6 WEB).

After a brief rain shower, the sun broke through the clouds. I sat with my face tilted toward the sun while warmth and light caressed my skin. Around me, my flower friends also tilted their petaled faces skyward. We smiled as sun shone upon us.

I pondered the Scripture about the Lord's face shining upon me. What did it mean? I recalled times when I rejoiced in the sunshine of God's blessings. Then, I recalled times when rain clouded my life. Was God's face not shining upon me during those times?

My flower friends knew the answer. Sunlight helps them create food, while rain helps them drink up nutrients from the soil. God's blessings come from both sun and rain.

My daughter Christine and her new husband PK were buying their first house. They were excited because they found a house they loved at a price they could afford. They basked in the sunshine of God's blessing. A few days before closing on the house, they discovered some serious problems in the house and the neighborhood. They had experts inspect the house. The reports were worse than expected, and Chris and PK were heartbroken. They cancelled their contract. As they shared their story, they concluded that giving up the house was actually a blessing. They could have bought the house and then discovered the problems. The Lord's face was shining upon them through their cloud of disappointment.

Joseph was a man who experienced sunshine and rain throughout his life. He was one of Jacob's twelve sons. Jacob loved Joseph more than any of his other sons. He gave him a

98

beautiful coat of many colors. Joseph glowed in his father's love; however, his bright days turned dark when his jealous brothers stripped off his coat and threw him into a pit.

Later, Joseph's brothers sold him to a traveling merchant. The merchant sold Joseph to an Egyptian man named Potiphar. As a servant to Potiphar, Joseph was well favored. He felt the Lord's face shining upon him once again.

That light turned dark when Potiphar's wife made false accusations against him and had Joseph thrown into prison, but "Yahweh was with Joseph and showed kindness to him, and gave him favor in the sight of the keeper of the prison" (Genesis 39:21 WEB). A sliver of light split his darkness.

During his prison term, Joseph became known for his gift of interpreting dreams. His gift brought him into Pharaoh's presence. When Joseph accurately interpreted Pharaoh's dreams, Pharaoh released him from prison and promoted him to the highest office in the kingdom. Because of his high position, Joseph was able to save his father and brothers from a terrible famine by bringing them to live with him in Egypt. Joseph understood that God's face had been shining upon him through all the hardship he suffered. Joseph comforted his guilt-ridden brothers by saying, "So now, it wasn't you who sent me here, but God" (Genesis 45:8 WEB).

Joseph discovered what the flowers know; the Lord's face shines upon us in sunshine and rain. When hardships knock us down, we can run to the Lord's arms where we soak up the nourishment that comes from being in his presence. Our spirits thrive during those times of closeness. With our faces nestled into our Heavenly Father's chest, we learn there can be joy in the midst of despair. We discover we can feel safe even though danger surrounds us. The Lord doesn't turn his face away from us in our hard times; he holds us close as he works in them to bring about good.

Time and again, rain clouds cover the sunshine in our lives. When they do, we run to the Lord for comfort and shelter. It's when we're encircled by the Lord's arms that we look up. Then, we see the light of his face shining upon us.

O Lord, help us to see your face glowing through our clouds.

Precious one, I'm always watching over you.

A MOMENT OF REFLECTION

Write about a time when you felt the Lord's face shining through your rain.

Hill Top Executive Course

Twenty-Six

Exploring a New Land

"We came to the land where you sent us. Surely it flows with milk and honey, and this is its fruit" (Numbers 13:27 WEB).

In the shade of a crepe myrtle tree, I look across the expanse of Hill Top Executive Course. Before me are rolling hills speckled with greens, tees, and sand traps. At the bottom of the hill, a fountain spouts from the middle of a lake. Sun diamonds dance over the rippling water. The vista is magnificent.

When my husband and I were making a decision about where to live after we retired, we discussed leaving our familiar surroundings and exploring options in a new state. We both grew up in New Jersey, so we had deep roots there. Our three children were married and settled there. Many of our friends and relatives lived locally. The home in which we raised our children held thirty-four years of memories. There was a strong pull to stay in New Jersey, but we felt a stronger desire to explore a new place. We struggled with conflicting emotions as we tried to make our decision.

In the thirteenth chapter of the book of Numbers, we read of a time when the nation of Israel struggled with conflicting emotions. Moses had been leading the people toward their promised homeland, a land flowing with milk and honey. After escaping from Egypt and traveling through the wilderness for many years, they were almost there. Moses sent men to scout out the land.

At the end of forty days, the scouts returned from their exploration. They reported the land was truly flowing with milk and honey. They even had samples of the luscious fruit growing on the trees, *but...*

The people clung to the word *but*. They agreed the land was good, *but* they said the current inhabitants of the land were powerful. They lived in large, fortified cities. Israel's promised homeland was within their grasp, *but* they clung to their fears.

How often do we miss out on wonderful opportunities because we cling to our fears and doubts? We see potential for something new or better, then we say *but*.

My husband and I saw the possibility of an exciting retirement, but it would require us to leave the familiarity and comfort of a place we'd lived most of our lives. We could try something new, but it meant moving away from our home, our friends, and family.

By refusing to take hold of their dream, Israel rebelled against God. He had great plans for them and they refused to participate in them. Their punishment was never to enter the Promised Land. That timid generation of Israel was sentenced to wander in the wilderness outside the borders of their homeland, never partaking of the goodness God had for them. Only the next generation would be allowed to claim the promise.

My husband and I felt strongly that we should move. Some people didn't understand our decision, and we had to be bold to follow through. We wanted to explore a land flowing with milk and honey.

In our new community we've developed friendships with wonderful people. We're pursuing activities we never had the opportunity to experience. Our new lifestyle provides me with time and inspiration to pursue my dream of writing. We've discovered creative ways to hold onto our ties in New Jersey, and we're enjoying the blessings of living in a new place.

Maybe the Lord has stirred your heart to stretch beyond your comfort zone. It may be a decision about where to live, or a nudge to undertake a new venture. You have the choice to explore a new land, or you can choose to remain where you feel comfortable. If you ignore the Lord's nudge, you'll have regrets. You will always wonder what could have been. Blessings come when we grab hold of the opportunities the Lord places before us.

O Lord, give us courage to take the first step.

Little one, taste the milk and honey of my plans.

A MOMENT OF REFLECTION

What is the Lord asking you to do that requires you to be bold and to stretch beyond what you or others expect? Write a prayer asking for courage to take the first step.

Village of Charlotte Entrance

Twenty-Seven

The Blessing of Rain

"Who covers the sky with clouds, who prepares rain for the earth, who makes grass grow on the mountain" (Psalm 147:8 WEB).

Rain refreshes the gardens and satisfies the thirsty ground. Vibrant flowers, glistening with water droplets, stand taller as they wiggle their roots into the moist sweet soil.

After a period of dry weather, I welcome the rain. It revives the plants and the lawn. The air, so pure and clean, invigorates me. I love to walk outside in the freshness of a rain shower.

The Lord uses rain as a testimony to his goodness. Without rain, crops would shrivel and die. The earth would dry up and nothing could flourish on it. Even the deserts rely on rain to perpetuate life. They receive no more than ten inches of rain a year, but when the clouds open up, the deserts experience a brief period of abundance, enough to sustain them through the long arid season.

Psalm 65 talks about the blessings of rain. It softens the ground so man can plow furrows and plant seeds. It fills streams that provide water to irrigate crops. Flocks and herds feed on the grasses that flourish in rain.

During his missionary journeys, the Apostle Paul used rain to testify to God's goodness. When he visited the city of Lystra, he came upon a crippled man and healed him. When the crowd saw the miracle Paul had performed, they ran toward Paul shouting that he was a god come to earth. They wanted to worship him, but Paul stopped them. He tried to reason with the excited mob, explaining he was only a man bringing good news about the living God. He said the God he worships made heaven and earth.

After calming the mob, Paul continued to explain that in times past, the Lord allowed nations to go their own ways, but even during those times he left his testimony upon mankind so they could know him. The Lord revealed his kindness to mankind by providing rain so the nations would have crops and food. Paul told the crowd he had come to their city to tell about the one true God who causes rain to fall upon the earth.

Jesus uses the example of rain to teach us how to behave toward our enemies. We are to love them and pray for them. Doing so proves we are sons of our Father in heaven. Jesus tells us his Father sends rain on both the righteous and unrighteous.

Rain is a gift from heaven. It causes us to look toward the sky and acknowledge the Creator of rain. As we observe the rain falling upon everyone, we're reminded of how we should treat others, showing kindness and sharing blessings with each person we meet. The Lord faithfully sends rain upon the entire earth to bless people of all races and nationalities. He even sends rain upon people who don't acknowledge him. The Lord's goodness spreads over all the earth. He wants us to follow his example in our interactions with others.

The Lord blesses the earth with rain, but he also rains extra blessings upon those who love him. The prophet Malachi admonished the Israelites to offer their full tithe to the Lord. Doing so was an act of obedience and reverence. It showed they acknowledged God's omnipotence and his ability to provide for all their needs. The Lord challenged them to test him and let him prove how many blessings he would pour over them, "that there shall not be room enough to receive it" (Malachi 3:10 ASV).

Our God pours rain and blessings over us. In return, he wants us to love him with all of our heart, soul, strength and mind. Our Lord wants us to prove that we trust him to provide for all of our needs by offering him a tithe of all we have.

O Lord, we are amazed by your goodness.

My child, I desire to rain abundant blessings upon you.

A MOMENT OF REFLECTION

What do you like most about the rain? In what ways do you see rain as a blessing from the Lord?

Starbucks Pergola

Twenty-Eight

A Lovely Fragrance

"Now thanks be to God, who always leads us in triumph in Christ and reveals through us the sweet aroma of his knowledge in every place" (2 Corinthians 2:14 WEB).

Like a colorful scarf, flowering vines wrap around the poles of the pergola behind Starbucks. Their airy fragrance wisps past my nose when I walk by, a sweet surprise.

Smells play a powerful role in our lives. They punctuate experiences and trigger memories. They reach us at a deeper level than sights and sounds. They penetrate the fibers of our beings and create an array of memories we associate with particular smells.

I remember the scent of my father's cologne. He wore Old Spice, and its scent clung to my hair and clothes when he hugged me. To this day, when I smell Old Spice it stirs up memories of my dad.

The scent of balsam reminds me of a place I visit in Maine. I love the sweet smell that permeates the woods. Last summer, I bought a pillow stuffed with balsam needles and I took it to my home in Florida. When I hold it to my nose, the fragrance stirs up memories of Maine.

When I breathe in the aroma of chocolate chip cookies, I remember the entire experience of mixing and baking cookies with my daughters, of eating raw cookie dough with our fingers, of laughing and talking while we wait for the cookies to come out of the oven. I visualize melted chocolate dripping from the warm cookies as we break off pieces to eat. That one smell stirs up years of memories.

More pleasing than the best aroma is the fragrance of Christ. It wafts from the hearts of those who love him, and it transfers to us through their acts of love.

My sister loves the Lord with all of her heart. One year when I went through a difficult time, she misted me with the sweet perfume of Christ. Her kind hospitality and sincere prayers refreshed my spirit, and I left her home stronger than when I arrived. Her acts of love sprayed the fragrance of Christ around me.

The Apostle Paul wrote letters to the newly formed churches to instruct and encourage the new believers. His letters, which we have in the New Testament, were scented with the fragrance of the Lord. All who read them were blessed, and the blessing carries to us today.

Aromas, odors, and fragrances cling to us, reflecting what we're near. In order to emanate the sweet perfume of Christ, we must stay close to him. The closer we nestle into him, the more his scent transfers to us. When we saturate our minds with his words, our thoughts reflect his thoughts. His truth purifies our motives. Our words and deeds begin to resemble his goodness.

If we claim to be a Christian but we don't spend time in the Lord's presence, instead of his fragrance, we carry our own scent with us. When we interact with others, they hear our words rather than the Lord's. Our deeds spring from our motives instead of those of Christ. The fragrance surrounding us lacks the pure essence of the Savior.

As Christians, we have the privilege, as well as the responsibility to spread the fragrance of the knowledge of Christ everywhere we go. We can't do that unless we carry the Lord's words inside our hearts. The words of our Savior soak into us while we read the Bible and meditate on the message of the Scriptures. As we kneel beside the Lord in prayer, his cologne clings to our hair and clothes so that people smell it on us. As we interact with others, they detect the fragrance of the Lord in our words and actions. If we want to give glory to our Lord, we need to be certain that the perfume surrounding us is his pure essence.

As we share our lives with others, we spread the fragrance of Christ everywhere we go.

O Lord, wash us with your lovely fragrance.

Precious one, devote yourself to being close to me.

A MOMENT OF REFLECTION

How has someone shared the fragrance of Christ with you? Write about the experience.

Paradise Exercise Park

Twenty-Nine

Strength to Strength

"Blessed are those whose strength is in you, who have set their hearts on pilgrimage. They go from strength to strength" (Psalm 84:5, 7 WEB).

Those who set their hearts on strengthening their muscles find a place to do that on the exercise machines at Paradise Park. It's set up as a circuit of machines, each one targeting a different muscle group. By following a regular workout routine, one's muscles become toned and strong.

My friend Tammy regularly exercises her faith muscles. She faces many struggles on a daily basis. When others would faint or give up, she perseveres. Her faith muscles increase as she relies upon divine fortitude to carry her through each challenge. Every time she trusts God to help her, her faith grows stronger. The Lord carries her from strength to strength as she goes through the circuit of her life.

We all face difficult challenges from time to time. When we face them in the arms of Jesus, our experience is very different than facing them in our own strength. With Jesus, we have hope because he is our divine source of power. We don't have to carry our burdens alone. The Lord carries us when we are weak.

Job was a man in the Bible whose faith muscles helped him go from strength to strength. He was wealthy and respected by all who knew him. In one day, calamity struck. His children died in a fatal accident, and he lost all his wealth. Despite the tragedy he suffered, Job still worshipped the Lord.

After that trouble passed, Job developed painful sores that covered his body. His wife told him to curse God and die, but Job still worshipped and trusted in the Lord.

During Job's terrible ordeal, three friends came to visit him. They blamed him for his troubles, accusing him of wrongdoing and sins he must not have confessed. Job's faith muscles remained strong enough to withstand their continual assault.

Job's unwavering faith in God's character helped him when he couldn't understand why he had to endure such suffering. In his physical and emotional weakness, Job relied on the Lord to carry him from strength to strength. In the end, the Lord blessed the latter part of Job's life more than the first.

Most of us will never experience suffering to the extent Job did, but without a strong faith, any suffering can overwhelm us. Strong faith muscles help us endure difficult times.

Paul understood the importance of exercising our faith muscles. He said we need to maintain our faith so when we're tested we can stand up to the test. He compared it to training for a race. Runners work hard, hoping to win a trophy. As Christians, we train to win an eternal prize. We train ourselves to maintain a strong faith so we can withstand the challenges life throws at us. If we regularly trust God in the little things, our faith will help us trust him when the big things hit us. Just as an athlete builds his muscles by continually lifting heavier weights, we increase our faith by continually trusting the Lord with more and more.

Knowing God's character helps us trust him. We come to know the Lord by spending time with him, by reading his word and by testing him when problems arise. Our Heavenly Father wants us to trust him. We're not meant to go through life in our own strength. We have access to divine power that is more than sufficient to help us over any obstacle.

Psalm 84 tells us that those who find their strength in the Lord are blessed. My friend Tammy is blessed as she relies on the Lord to help her in her daily struggles. She is blessed when she rests in his arms.

The Lord carries us when we grow weary. He holds us up with his mighty hands until we're able to stand. When we trust our Lord, he carries us from strength to strength.

Heavenly Father, we rely on you to help us through our challenges.

Little one, lean on me. I am your source of strength.

A MOMENT OF REFLECTION

When confronted with challenges, is your first instinct to trust the Lord? How can you increase your faith muscles?

Covered Bridge at Lake Sumter Landing

Thirty

Praising the Lord

*"Praise Yahweh, all you works of his, in all places of his dominion.
Praise Yahweh, my soul" (Psalm 103:22 WEB).*

Like small paddleboats, ducks churn through the water, creating ripples in their wakes. With a mighty rush, they flap their wings and skirt tippy-toe across the pond's surface to take flight, then skid feet-first as they land.

In the shade of the covered bridge, I marvel at the works of the Lord. Below the bridge, fish shimmer as sunbeams dive into the water and bounce off their silvery scales. Black-eyed Susans and plumbagos paint the stream bank with splashes of orange and blue. The stream gurgles, and the grasses rustle. The works of the Lord fill my senses. I'm in the middle of nature's concert of praise to the Creator.

When ducks swim, flowers bloom, and streams gurgle, they are praising the Lord by being what the Lord created them to be, and by doing what they were created to do. God gave all of creation the ability to praise him. Isaiah 55 tells us the mountains and hills will sing, and the trees will clap their hands. The cycle of nature praises the Lord by doing what God purposed it to do. Rain and snow water the earth so the earth can nourish plants, which flower and yield seed. Seed produces food and grain, which are used to feed man. Each part of the cycle glorifies God.

Psalm 104 describes more ways in which creation praises the Lord. The moon brightens the night and marks off seasons. Lions roar for their prey, trusting God to supply it. All creatures look to the Lord to provide their needs. Dependence on their Maker is a form of praise. Everything in creation praises God through its very being and its need of his care.

Mankind praises the Lord in many different ways. When the tabernacle was set up as a place of worship for Israel, certain men were chosen to be singers before the Lord. Our Heavenly Father desires to hear us singing, using the voices he created within us. In fact, in Ephesians 5:19 we are commanded to sing and make music in our hearts.

The Lord also delights in the sound of instruments. Psalm 150 tells us to praise the Lord with harps and lyres; with trumpets, flutes and stringed instruments; even with tambourines and cymbals.

Dancing is also a form of praise. Miriam, the sister of Moses, led the women in dancing with tambourines to praise God for delivering them from captivity in Egypt. David danced before the Ark of the Covenant as it was being carried into the city of Jerusalem. 2 Samuel 6:14 tells us he leaped and danced with all his might.

I dance hula, and I was pleased to learn that hula is used as a form of praising God in many Christian churches in Hawaii and other states. Teachers of hula choreograph dances to worship songs. Graceful and beautiful, these hulas glorify the Lord and touch the audience in a way that brings tears to their eyes. I've been blessed to be part of such a performance.

We were created with hearts that desire to praise, and we were created to offer praise. The Lord loves to receive our pure passionate praise, be it through singing, playing an instrument, or dancing before him.

We also offer praise through the work of our hands. We were all blessed with unique abilities. We're told in Colossians 3:17 to use all that we do as an act of praise to the Lord. Our words, our deeds, our talents, our gifts, and our abilities allow us to glorify God. When we offer all that we are and all that we have to the Lord, it is our offering of praise to the Almighty. "Let everything that has breath praise the Lord. Praise the Lord" (Psalm 150:6 NIV).

O Lord, we desire to praise you with our whole being.

Child, your acts of praise make me smile.

A MOMENT OF REFLECTION

How can you use your uniqueness as an offering of praise to the Lord?

Eisenhower Recreation Center

Thirty-One

The Gift of Sacrifice

"Greater love has no one than this, that someone lay down his life for his friends" (John 15:13 WEB).

An American flag waves high above a circle of monuments at the entrance to Eisenhower Recreation Center. The monuments honor each branch of the military and remind us of Americans who sacrificed for their countrymen. Inside the recreation center are memorabilia honoring those who served during various wars. Some of the soldiers gave their lives to protect something greater than themselves.

Not only did soldiers pay the price of sacrifice, their families also felt the cost. Parents, spouses, and siblings who lost loved ones know the pain of sacrifice.

There are many careers that place people in harm's way. Besides the military, there are firefighters, rescue workers, and those in law enforcement. The very nature of their job is to run toward danger. When these people leave for work each day, they know there's a possibility they won't return home that night, but they're willing to face danger to save lives. People who are willing to sacrifice their lives to save others carry a divine instinct within them, a spark that must come from the Lord.

Sacrifice is a selfless act done to benefit another. Although we usually think of it in terms of the careers discussed above, it also occurs in more subtle ways. Regular people make sacrifices to enrich the lives of others. A teacher uses her lunch break to help a struggling student. A father gives up his one day off from work to coach his son's baseball team. A neighbor offers her time and resources to help a neighbor in need. Each one of these acts requires the giver to make a sacrifice to help another.

On a daily basis, mothers sacrifice their time for their children. As I watch my daughters, I feel a sense of pride. They juggle more than I ever had to as a young mother. They work full time while raising active children. Their days begin as soon as their children wake up. Their primary focus, no matter what else they have to do, is the well-being of their children. My daughters work tirelessly well beyond their children's bedtimes. They're lucky to find fifteen minutes in a day to do something for themselves. They sacrifice themselves in order to care for their children.

Motherhood is an all-consuming calling. Mothers exhibit godly qualities as they devote their lives to their children. I believe the mothering instinct gives us a glimpse into the kind of devotion our Savior has for us.

Sacrifice in any form involves a cost. The one offering the sacrifice gives up something valuable for the sake of another. In the Old Testament, a lamb was sacrificed to atone for the sins of the people. The lamb was to be the firstborn and without spot or blemish. The lamb was completely innocent. Its blood was accepted as a substitute for the sinner's blood. The lamb's life was sacrificed to benefit sinful man. This system of animal sacrifice was in place until God's perfect plan was carried out.

Jesus was the perfect Lamb of God. He was God's first-born Son, holy and pure without spot or blemish. He committed no sin. The crucifixion of Jesus Christ was the greatest sacrifice ever offered. God the Father suffered the pain of giving up his only Son for our sakes. We were unworthy and rebellious, mired in sin, but God's love was so great he wanted to save us from eternal separation from him. He sent Jesus to bear the punishment we deserved. Jesus willingly died in our place because he loved us. Our Lord and Savior paid the ultimate price by sacrificing his life for us.

As we think of those who serve others through their jobs, and as we think of those who gave all for their countrymen, let's remember the One who gave all for our souls.

Most High God, may we never take for granted the sweet gift of sacrifice.

Child, it is finished. My Son gave all.

A MOMENT OF REFLECTION

Think of those who sacrificed something for you. Write an acknowledgement of their sweet gift, then bow your head and thank the Lord for his amazing gift of sacrifice.

Moving Clouds

Thirty-Two

Change

"So God created Man in his own image, in the image of God created he him; male and female created he them" (Genesis 1:27 DARBY).

Like chalk blown across a sketchpad, cottony wisps float across the expanse of sky. Clouds morph into new dream pictures as air currents glide through them. Mountains drift into oceans, which change into deserts. Continuously clustering and stretching, clouds form new pictures minute by minute.

The clouds remind me I'm in a continual process of change. God has a perfect design planned for me. Through the Holy Spirit he glides through my spirit, causing small subtle changes in my attitude, my values, and my priorities. Each change moves me closer to becoming the person I was created to be.

When God made the world, he did it through a process of continuous change. We read the story of creation in the book of Genesis. Beginning with a dark void, the Lord created light and separated it from the darkness. Next, he created an expanse he called sky. It separated the waters above from the waters below. On the third day, the Lord gathered the waters below into seas. He formed land and filled it with vegetation. The sun, moon, and stars appeared on the fourth day to designate times and seasons. On the fifth day, the sky and seas teemed with life. The sixth day, God filled the land with living creatures. Lastly, he created man in his own image. Each change occurred until the Lord completed his masterpiece we call earth. "God saw everything that he had made, and behold it was very good" (Genesis 1:31 DARBY).

The Heavenly Father has a master plan for our lives, too. Over time, he breathes across our lives, gradually moving us toward his vision. Sometimes, he allows blatant changes to jolt us from our steady paths.

I know people from a recovery group in my former church. They followed a path of self-indulgence and addiction until a jolt brought them to their knees. It may have been an arrest or a spouse threatening to leave, but it caused them to stop and reevaluate the path they were on. Many of them sought help so they could change paths. In the recovery group, they learned about the Savior, and gradually the Lord caused beautiful changes in them.

A famous example of change is George Foreman. During his early boxing career, he was an aggressive, violent fighter. In the famous fight known as "The Rumble in the Jungle," George Foreman savagely pounded Muhammad Ali. Foreman was a fierce and frightening man until the Lord gently blew across him, changing him from a wild beast into a gentle Christian husband and father. Today, he's famous for his product known as the Foreman Grill.

The work of God is powerful. Not only does it cause changes in people's hearts, it causes changes in people's situations. Our lot in life and our circumstances are not permanent. Like the clouds, they're always in a process of variation. We may think we're stuck in a situation that will never get any better, but if we trust in the Lord, he will alter things in his perfect timing.

Often, the Lord's plans aren't apparent to us. Invisibly, he works in our hearts and the hearts of others as he creates beautiful designs in the landscapes of our lives. We don't notice the revisions until we look back over the years. Each breath of divine air moves the filaments of our lives closer to God's design. Even when we smudge our pictures, our Heavenly Father blows the chalk to change our smudges into something good. Such modifications take a lifetime, but the Lord continues to work in us until he creates his masterpiece.

Paul prayed, "being confident of this very thing, that he who began a good work in you will complete it until the day of Jesus Christ" (Philippians 1:6 WEB).

Heavenly Father, when we look at the clouds, help us remember you are always working in our lives to create something beautiful.

Little one, I will complete the good work I began in you.

A MOMENT OF REFLECTION

Can you recall a subtle or not-so-subtle change the Lord caused in your life? Write about it.

Creekside Stream

Thirty-Three

Empty Hands

"I went away full, but Jehovah has brought me home again empty" (Ruth 1:21 DARBY).

A path winds lazily beside a gurgling stream. Ferns reach outspread fingers toward the sun, as if asking God to fill their empty hands.

I stroll the path along Creekside Stream. Thousands of ferns crowd the banks. Their leaves resemble hands reaching toward God. I think about my hands. Are they tightly clenched, or are they open to the Lord?

The book of Ruth is a story of full and empty hands. There was a famine in the land of Israel when a woman named Naomi, her husband, and two sons left for the land of Moab, where they'd heard there was food. While living there, Naomi's hands were full. She had her family and enough food for them to eat. Then her husband died. A while after that, her sons violated God's law by marrying Moabite women. Ten years later, the sons both died. Naomi's full hands were empty. With a sad heart, she returned to her homeland. She told the townspeople no longer to call her Naomi, but to call her Mara, which means "bitter."

Little by little, the Lord showed his faithfulness by restoring Naomi's blessings. Her daughter-in-law Ruth accompanied Naomi to her homeland. Naomi had taught Ruth about the one true God, and Ruth worshipped the Lord. Ruth wanted to care for her mother-in-law. Each day, Ruth went to the fields to gather bits of grain left behind by the farm workers. The grain sustained her and Naomi.

While Ruth worked, a landowner named Boaz noticed her good character. He admired her and inquired about her. Boaz discovered she was the widow of one of his kinsmen. According to Jewish law, a relative was to marry his kinsman's widow.

Boaz married Ruth, and their marriage secured Naomi's care for her old age. Ruth and Boaz had a son who became the grandfather of King David. The Lord filled Naomi's empty hands with more blessings than she could have imagined.

The Lord wants to fill our hands with blessings, but sometimes we take our blessings for granted. Through our own foolish negligence, they may slip from our hands. One day, we may look for all we had and find it is gone.

It could be that we didn't value our good health. We ate the wrong foods and neglected to exercise regularly. One day, we realize we can't do what we used to do, and we have to work to regain the abilities we once had.

We all know stories of relationships that fall apart because one or both parties don't appreciate the value of each other. Only when one person is gone does the other person realize what is lost. Once full hands are empty.

Sometimes, our hands are so full of worldly things there's no room for the blessings God has for us. Our hands may be spilling over with fruitless activities or vain pursuits. Our plans take up all the space. The Lord may need to pry open our tightly clasped hands so our plans spill out and allow room for his.

There are countless stories of famous individuals who crash from their high pinnacles. It's a humbling experience. For some people, it takes losing their fame and fortune before they open themselves up to the Lord.

Through no fault of our own, blessings may be snatched from our hands. Like Naomi, we may become bitter. We can remain bitter, or we can reach our empty hands to the Lord and ask him to fill them.

Emptiness is a temporary condition for God's children. He desires to bless us abundantly. He provides sustenance for our needs. He replaces our sadness with joy, our repentance with forgiveness and our loneliness with his Presence. When we stretch empty hands to our Heavenly Father, he fills them with more blessings than we could ever imagine.

O Lord, we lift empty hands to you.

Precious one, I desire to pour my blessings into your outstretched hands.

A MOMENT OF REFLECTION

Are your hands full? Examine the contents to see what's filling them. Are your hands empty? Lift them to the Lord so he can fill them.

Hospice House Courtyard

Thirty-Four

Bittersweet Memories

"...and the waters were made sweet" (Exodus 15:25 WEB).

Emotions swirl through me like cumulus clouds swirl in the sky above me. Memories blow against me like a persistent breeze.

As I stand in the hospice courtyard, I think of my parents and in-laws who passed from this life to their eternal homes. I recall happy times we shared. I remember their words as I visualize their eyes and their smiles. My father always called me his "beautiful redhead." I wear those words like a charm around my neck. His unconditional love gave me confidence in myself. It's amazing how a small phrase can influence a child.

My mother taught me about hospitality. She was the most gracious host I've ever known. She welcomed everyone into our home and always prepared a delicious meal.

I learned about organization from my mother-in-law. She even organized her junk drawer. Her example inspired me to keep my house neat and tidy.

Whenever I pass a fruit stand, I think of my father-in-law. Once a week, he bought fresh fruit for his granddaughters. He got a kick out of watching the juice dribble down their chins as they bit into a ripe, juicy piece of fruit. Some of the memories of my loved ones make me laugh. I miss them tremendously.

I also remember my regrets, words I wish I'd said or hadn't said, things I wish hadn't occurred. Since the opportunity to right any wrongs is gone, my memories are both bitter and sweet. They hold feelings of joy and pain.

In chapter three of James, the author discusses the hypocrisy of our tongues. The tongue is the most powerful member of the body because it spouts out words that leave a lasting impression upon the hearer. Both bitter and sweet words proceed from the same mouth. James says that shouldn't be.

I allowed my tongue to ramble, speaking words I lament today. I also withheld words I should've spoken. Because of my undisciplined tongue, my memories are both joyful and regretful. Bitter memories are difficult. We can't change what's already happened, but neither can we allow the sour taste of our memories to pollute our present. Remorse for something we can't change causes our sweetness to turn. Then our ugly disposition affects those around us. How can we release the bitterness within?

While Moses was leading Israel to the Promised Land, they came to the Desert of Shur. The people trudged across the dry dusty sand, unable to find any water. Finally, after three days, they found water, but they couldn't drink it because it was bitter.

Frustration and anger simmered in the people and bubbled over. They took it out on Moses. He cried out to the Lord asking what he should do. The Lord instructed Moses to throw a piece of wood into the water. When Moses threw in the wood, the bitter water became sweet and the people could drink it.

The Lord sweetened the bitter water for the Israelites, and he can sweeten the bitter taste of our regrets. He won't change our memories, but he can alter their potency. We have a piece of wood known as the cross of Jesus. When we lay our remorse at the foot of the cross, Jesus will forgive the words and actions we confess. His forgiveness is sweetness to our spirits.

We need the Lord's comfort as we navigate the emotions of losing loved ones. Praise be to God, the Father of compassion, the God of all comfort. When we share our regrets with him, he soothes us. He fills the void of our loneliness with his Presence. Our Heavenly Father wraps us in softness and heals our hurting spirits. He renews us so we become emotionally strong and healthy. Then our Father sends us out to comfort others with the comfort we received from him.

O Lord, we reach up for your comfort.

Come to me, little one, I'll wipe away each teardrop from your eyes.

A MOMENT OF REFLECTION

Do you wrestle with bitter memories? Write them down and lay them before the Lord, then drink deeply of the sweet forgiveness he provides.

Havana Hemingway Course

Thirty-Five

The Secret of Contentment

"I know how to be humbled, and I know also how to abound. In everything and in all things I have learned the secret both to be filled and to be hungry, both to abound and to be in need" (Philippians 4:12 WEB).

Mounds of periwinkle flowers cluster along the path and quiver in the breeze. Clouds smear the sky like feather-brushed whipped cream. In this downy setting, I feel contentment drape around me like a soft quilt.

As a child, I experienced contentment in my parents' love. It didn't matter to me that our car wasn't new or my clothes were homemade. My parents' love was the source of my happiness, and their love satisfied me completely.

As I grew older, I continued to be grateful for simple things. My father taught school, and my mother stayed home with the children. We spent our summers living in a tent at a campground my father managed. In the evening, we caught toads and sang around the campfire. Life was simple and fun for my brother and me. For most of my school years, I was happy with my life. I didn't desire things outside of my family's budget. I was grateful for what I had.

A sense of discontentment began nibbling at me in my twenties. I was searching for something more, but I didn't know what that was. I discovered it in a tent in Nevada.

My then-boyfriend (now husband) and I joined the free-spirit, hippie lifestyle of the 70's, and we hitchhiked across the country. I struggled with an empty feeling that increased the day we met some people from a counter-culture group. Their propaganda stirred up many questions and doubts within me. I was discontented the rest of the day.

That night while I was alone in a tent, I sensed the Lord's Presence. In a brief moment, he revealed my sins to me. I knew I needed his mercy. In my shame and brokenness, I asked for forgiveness. Jesus assured me I was covered by his grace. He washed me with mercy and wrapped me in his love. My life changed that night. I found lasting contentment in God's amazing love.

We may go through a period of discontentedness before we find contentment. Discontentedness takes two forms. One type prompts us to make a change. It acts as an impetus to push us forward. It may move us toward a spiritual change.

The other type of discontentedness turns us away from God and moves us toward despair. We focus on the negative. We're always dissatisfied with something: our appearance, our spouse, our status, our lack of possessions. We become ungrateful, always wanting something more, bigger, or better. We believe the lie that whispers, "If only ____ was different, I'd be happy."

When we become chronically discontented, temptations slither into our lives and lure us to seek false happiness in unhealthy activities. Chronic discontentedness drives us away from God and blinds us to our blessings.

King Solomon understood the vanity of trying to satisfy a discontented spirit through self-indulgence. In the book of Ecclesiastes, after evaluating man's futile attempts at finding contentment, he concludes, "This is the end of the matter. All has been heard. Fear God, and keep his commandments; for this is the whole duty of man" (Ecclesiastes 12:13 WEB).

The Apostle Paul claimed to know the secret of contentment. He was beaten, imprisoned, and bound with chains for preaching about Jesus; yet even in his suffering, he was at peace. Paul sought his happiness in the Lord, not circumstances. We discover Paul's secret of contentment when the Lord becomes everything to us. Only Jesus satisfies our deepest needs. The world's rewards disappoint and fade away, but the love of our Lord lasts forever. Being satisfied in the Lord is the secret of contentment.

Lord, only you bring lasting satisfaction.

Precious one, be content in my fullness.

A MOMENT OF REFLECTION

Are you content or do you to feel chronically discontented? Change your perspective by listing the many blessings you have. Thank God for all he gives you.

Paradise Grove Park Walking Path

Thirty-Six

Nesting by the Blessings

"The birds of heaven dwell by them; they give forth their voice from among the branches. He watereth the mountains from his upper chambers: the earth is satisfied with the fruit of thy works" (Psalm 104:12-13 DARBY).

Birds twitter from the trees by the lake while ducks sail across the water. On a nearby island, geese gather in a noisy gaggle. They all seem satisfied as they nest by the water.

In Psalm 104, the psalmist proclaims the earth is satisfied by the blessings God pours over it. Enjoying the lakeside garden at Paradise Park, I agree with him. The flowers, shrubs, and wildlife attest to the earth's jubilant response to the Lord's goodness.

As I stroll the walking path through Paradise Park, I think about my satisfaction meter. Is it registering as high as it should? I have good health, a loving family, and financial security. My satisfaction level should be steadily high, but I sense it fluctuating. My life isn't perfect. I have my share of problems, but I also have an abundance of blessings. I realize my level of satisfaction follows my thoughts. When I focus on my problems, I overlook my blessings and my joy decreases. If I look at the blessings, my attitude changes, even though my situation remains the same.

Helen H. Lemmel wrote a beautiful hymn entitled "Turn Your Eyes Upon Jesus." The lyrics tell us when we look into the face of Jesus, the things on earth grow dim. The author of Hebrews 12:2 tells us to fix our eyes on Jesus. The Scripture implies that we are in control of our eyes. We choose where we want to look. When we *fix* our eyes on Jesus, we direct our attention, our mind, and our thoughts steadily upon him. When we turn our eyes upon Jesus, he becomes the lens through which we view everything.

I am the executrix of a will for a loved one's estate. It's been a complicated process with some legal snags. When I look at the problems, I fill up with anxiety. If I refocus and fix my eyes unwaveringly upon Jesus, I calm down. The estate problems fade into the background of my vision. The situation doesn't change: My focus changes. The issues still need to be resolved, but as I look into the Lord's face, I know he will help me. Looking into the face of Jesus, I see his deity and I remember he is the one in control. I trust him to work things out for my good.

"Eye hath not seen, nor ear heard, neither has entered into the heart of man the things which God hath prepared for them that love him" (1Corinthians 2:9 KJV). We can't even imagine the blessings the Lord has for us. If we want to experience the satisfaction described by the psalmist, we need to look at the source of our satisfaction. We need to practice eye discipline.

When my husband was a little boy, one of his eyes turned inward. The doctor gave him eye exercises, and he had to wear a patch over his good eye to force his weak eye to look forward. The exercise worked and today he has 20/20 vision in both eyes.

During my stroll through Paradise Park, I discipline my eyes to look upward. As my focus holds steady on the Lord, a sense of peace and satisfaction washes over me.

Just as God waters the earth with his goodness, he pours blessings into our lives. However, if we don't look for the blessings, we may overlook them. When we learn to fix our eyes on Jesus, our blessings take the forefront and our problems dim. When our focus changes, our outlook brightens. We begin to weave our blessings into a nest where our thoughts can dwell. By turning our eyes upon the source of our blessings, we experience satisfaction deep in our spirits.

O Lord, we turn our eyes upon you so our thoughts can nest by our blessings.

Little one, my eyes steadily focus upon your well-being.

A MOMENT OF REFLECTION

Practice eye discipline today. Record your many blessings. Then check your satisfaction meter.

Stream Beside The Sharon

Thirty-Seven

Still and Quiet Waters

"Jehovah is my shepherd, I shall not want. He maketh me to lie down in green pastures; He leadeth me beside still waters. He restoreth my soul"
(Psalm 23:1-3 ASV).

In a quiet corner near the Sharon L. Morse Performing Arts Center, a stream trickles over stones as it flows along a shaded bank. The gentle gurgling sound soothes my spirit, and I think of green pastures and quiet waters.

I imagine sheep grazing by a stream as a loving shepherd watches over them. He guides them to clear cool water and guards them as they graze in green pastures. The sheep rest peacefully in their shepherd's care.

Sheep need a shepherd because they are easy prey for many predators. Their only defense mechanism is to flee, and they're not very fast. If a predator overtakes them, they can't effectively fight back.

David was a shepherd. He stayed in the pasture watching over his father's sheep. If a lion or bear threatened to attack, David fought it off with his sling. He was a faithful protector.

Sheep are vulnerable to other dangers besides predators. Left to themselves, they may nibble poisonous plants or drink polluted water. They may stray from the flock, wandering off and becoming lost. They need their shepherd's watchful care.

It's no wonder Jesus refers to himself as the Good Shepherd and to us as sheep. We are creatures who are vulnerable to spiritual predators. Our predators may be "wolves in sheep's clothing." Some of these predators lure us with deceitful words. Such predators may be religious people who misrepresent God's word. Our only defense is to know what is in the Bible so we can discern truth from falsehood.

A spiritual predator may also take the form of a temptation. A person or activity may seem desirable. It promises happiness; however, once we're ensnared, we realize all of its promises were lies. At that point we're like the sheep who nibbled poisonous plants or drank polluted water.

We may be a sheep who always follows the shepherd and stays within the safety of the flock. Then one day we wander away. Without our shepherd's guidance, we stumble into trouble and need to be rescued. Or, maybe we wander so far from the flock we get lost. Our only hope is for our loving shepherd to find us.

Jesus told a parable about a lost sheep. He said a man had a hundred sheep. One sheep wandered off and was lost. The man left the ninety-nine to search for the one lost sheep. When he found it, he carried it on his shoulders rejoicing. "I tell you that even so there will be more joy in heaven over one sinner who repents, than over ninety and nine righteous people who need no repentance" (Luke 15:7 WEB).

Jesus is our Good Shepherd. We're never lost to him because he's always watching over us. He desires to carry us on his shoulders and keep us in the safety of his pasture; however, he never forces us to go with him. Jesus wants to be our Good Shepherd, but he waits for us to choose him. Sheep recognize their shepherd's voice and respond only to him. Jesus calls to us and waits for us to respond to his voice.

A good shepherd risks his life to protect his sheep. Jesus, our faithful shepherd, willingly laid down his life for us, his sheep. There's no greater sacrifice than a life. Our Shepherd sacrificed his life to save us. Is there any logical reason we wouldn't respond to him?

When we see quiet, still waters, we can think of Jesus. When we see green pastures, we can think of Jesus. He'll always protect us, and he'll always watch over us. In the tender care of our Savior, we can be as content as sheep beside still waters.

O Lord, may we always be content beside the still waters of your Presence.

Little one, you are my precious lamb. I invite you to dwell with me forever.

A MOMENT OF REFLECTION

Do you identify with one of the sheep mentioned above? Write a prayer for rescue or a prayer for contentment.

Pond in the Village of Lake Deaton

Thirty-Eight

The Gift of Wisdom

"But if any of you lacks wisdom, let him ask of God, who gives to all liberally and without reproach; and it will be given to him" (James 1:5 WEB).

Like the silver beards of ancient sages, moss hangs from the branches of an aged oak tree. In the shade of this stately tree, I'm inspired to open my Bible to study the words of the Ancient of Days, the Creator of wisdom.

I read of King Solomon who was known for his wisdom. He wasn't born with it; it was a gift from the Lord. After Solomon inherited the throne of his father David, the Lord appeared to Solomon in a dream and told him to ask for anything he wanted. Solomon asked for wisdom so he could rule wisely over God's people. Jehovah was pleased with his request and promised to give Solomon a wise and discerning heart. The Lord promised that no one before or after Solomon would have as much wisdom as he had.

When I reflect upon my life, I wish I had been wiser. As I look back through the years, I see many foolish decisions. I wish I had been a wiser parent. I wish I had made wiser choices when opportunities arose, but wishing the past was different is a waste of time. I can't change history. What's done is done. What I can do is learn how to live wisely from this time forward.

The Bible says, "The fear of Yahweh is the beginning of wisdom" (Psalm 111:10 WEB). We don't even have a chance at being wise until we learn to fear the Lord. Fear refers to holy reverence. Fearing the Lord means honoring his will. It means showing reverence for our Maker. It fills us with a passion to worship and adore our Creator.

The main reason I made foolish choices was because I didn't fear the Lord. I didn't ask him to guide me. I trusted in my own counsel.

In the first chapter of the book of James, we learn that God generously gives us wisdom if we ask him for it. Solomon asked and he received. The gift of wisdom is ours if we simply ask. Not only is the Lord delighted to give us wisdom, but also he gives generously without finding fault. He doesn't begrudge our request or keep score of how many foolish decisions we've made in the past. The Lord requires one thing: When we ask, we must ask in faith. If we doubt, James tells us we're like a wave tossed about by the wind.

I asked for wisdom about how to proceed with my dream of writing, but I asked without actually believing the Lord would guide me. For years, I was blown and tossed like a wave. I would pray and then doubt, pray and doubt, never believing I could do anything meaningful with my writing. As a result, I didn't accomplish much.

After years of floundering, I finally asked in faith, believing the Lord would guide me. I desperately wanted to be a writer for the Lord. This time I trusted the Lord to give me wisdom about how to proceed.

When we ask in faith, the Lord shows us the way. He led me to a local writing group that helped me improve my skills. I received affirmation when I was published in several publications, and I won awards at a writing conference. This book is the result of asking for wisdom and believing the Lord is leading me.

Wisdom is a gift freely offered to us despite our history of foolish choices and half-hearted attempts. With the Lord, each moment is an opportunity for us to try again by pursuing wisdom. Our past doesn't determine our present. Our Heavenly Father offers us the gift of wisdom so we can live wisely. When we start at the beginning by fearing the Lord, he'll help us become wise sages who make good decisions.

Dear Lord, thank you for the amazing gift of wisdom.

Precious one, I delight in blessing you.

A MOMENT OF REFLECTION

In what ways have you come to the beginning of wisdom by fearing the Lord? Ask him for wisdom about specific things for which you need guidance, then record the answers you receive.

Killdeer Course

Thirty Nine

Living in Twilight

"For thou art my lamp, O Lord: and the Lord will lighten my darkness"
(2 Samuel 22:29 KJV).

The moon's diffused glow is the only source of light. Everything around me hides in shadows. Suddenly, golden fingers reach up and set the sky ablaze. Light pours over the earth and I can see clearly.

I like to walk at dawn, the time just before sunrise when everything is blurred in misty shadows. Because of the haze, I can't see clearly until the sun rises. My early morning walks remind me that my life is like a walk at dawn. I have limited understanding about happenings in the present, and I can't see into the future. Even the past lacks clarity. I live with fuzzy vision. So how can life make sense?

The Lord promises to be a light to guide me through the darkness. He asks me to trust him to lead me along my dimly lit path. I don't need to see everything or understand everything. I only need to see him. The Lord wants me to walk beside him. Only he can see clearly during the time I live in twilight.

One day, the vast unknown frightened me. I worried about what would happen if certain factors played out. I couldn't control the factors, and I certainly couldn't control their outcome. Anxiety wound my nerves into a tight string. Then I heard the Lord's voice in the writings of David. "For by thee I have run through a troop: by my God have I leaped over a wall" (2 Samuel 22:30 KJV). David said that no obstacle was too great for God. With the Lord's help, no problem was insurmountable. David trusted in God when circumstances seemed impossible.

In the same way, I only needed to look to the Lord to help my situation. I didn't need to understand everything, I only needed to see the Lord's hand holding onto my arm guiding me.

When children visit the doctor, they don't understand all the reasons behind their visit. They cling to their parents for comfort. They trust their parents to do what is best.

We are the Lord's children. We can't comprehend all that happens in our lives, but we can cling to our Heavenly Father for comfort. We can trust him to know what is best for us.

David faced terrifying situations. Enemies pursued him and wanted to end his life. He didn't know how things would turn out, but David trusted the Lord to manage his circumstances.

David lived in twilight like we do. He couldn't see what would happen in the misty future, but he kept his eyes on the Lord. David overcame his fears by looking to God, his rock, his fortress and his great deliverer.

We'll walk in the dimness of twilight as long as we live on earth. Then the day will come when we'll meet the Lord in heaven. On that day, light will pour over our understanding like an early morning sunrise. We'll understand why our prayers were answered as they were, why we had to experience certain situations. We'll comprehend that God tenderly cared for us even when things seemed to be going all wrong.

Until that time comes, the Lord offers his arm. He wants us to cling to him. He knows we feel lost in the shadows, so he promises to guide us. He tells us to rely on his insight when we're afraid of the unknown. He is the One who knows everything. The Lord sees light where we see only darkness. During our time we walk in twilight, the light we need comes from the Lord.

Heavenly Father, we rely on you with each step we take.

Precious one, I will light your way.

A MOMENT OF REFLECTION

Recall a Scripture or two that lit your way, or a moment when the Lord shone a light in your darkness. Write about it.

Rohan Recreation Center

Forty

Aged to Perfection

"Even the youths shall faint and be weary, and the young men shall stumble utterly and fall: but they that wait for Jehovah shall renew their strength, they shall mount up with wings as eagles" (Isaiah 40:30-31 ASV).

It circles high above the clouds. With dark, outstretched wings the eagle glides on the upper air currents. I watch it soar above Soaring Eagle Softball Complex. From its vantage point, the eagle can see more than I can.

I know it's an adult eagle by its coloring – brown-black wings, white head, and, if I could see them, piercing yellow eyes. It took five years for the eagle's feathers to take on their adult coloring. At each stage of maturity, its feathers changed. God planned the eagle's growth process so its feathers and coloring would suit its needs as it matured. This final phase is the most glorious.

Isn't that typical of our Heavenly Father to save the best for last? We go through many phases in our lives. The period from childhood to youth and from youth to young adult are our optimal learning stages. Then we enter our productive phase where we build families and careers. Eventually, we arrive at our final phase, our retirement years. By the time we reach this stage of life, we may think our best years are behind us. But with the Lord, this final phase can be our most glorious.

Many famous people from the Bible achieved their greatest accomplishments in their old age. Abraham was one hundred years old when his promised son Isaac was born. When God tested Abraham by asking him to sacrifice his only son, Abraham passed the test because his faith in God was so strong he was willing to obey the Lord's command. The Lord intervened and Isaac lived.

Moses was eighty years old when the Lord sent him to Egypt to rescue Israel from captivity.

Elizabeth was well along in years before her first child was born. We know him as John the Baptist, the cousin of Jesus.

Simeon and Anna were very old. They had been waiting a lifetime to see the promised Christ child. God granted them the privilege of not only seeing Jesus but of holding and blessing the tiny babe.

The Apostle Paul wrote many of his letters to the churches while he was an old man in prison.

God directed the churches to appoint elders to oversee his flock. He directed the older women to be examples to the younger women, training them how to be good wives and mothers.

By the time we reach retirement, we may think we had our chance to either succeed or fail in our endeavors. We may think it's our time to coast, but the Lord wants us to soar. We gained wisdom over the years. It came from our failures as much as our successes. Our Heavenly Father has an important purpose for us in our old age because we have much to share with the world. We have a lifetime of experiences, skills, and talents. If we submit them to the Lord, he can use them for his glory.

As we reflect over our past, we can see how we've made both good and bad choices. The Lord is always willing to offer forgiveness for the bad. We need only ask him. He doesn't want us weighed down by regrets as we move into our final phase. He wants us to experience hope, joy, comfort, and forgiveness. The Lord wants us to enter our final stage soaring above our past so we can be our most glorious selves. The Lord promises to give us the energy we need to accomplish his plans. Just as the eagle soars highest during its final stage of life, so we are meant to soar to our highest heights before the Lord gives us eternal rest.

Dear Lord, reveal your plans for us, and give us the energy to accomplish them for your glory.

Precious child, I will renew your strength so you can soar on wings like eagles.

A MOMENT OF REFLECTION

List gifts, talents, and valuable experiences you have, then ask the Lord to show you how he wants you to use them for his glory.

About the Author

Doris Hoover resides in The Villages, Florida. She also spends time along the coast of Maine. Her passion is discovering God's messages in nature and sharing them with others. She writes about the inspiration of nature on her website www.captivatedbythecreator.com.

Doris won awards for her devotionals and she's been published in The Upper Room, as well as two devotional books God Still Leads and Guides, and Light for the Writer's Soul. She shares photographs and writings about Maine on her website www.downeastmusings.com.

Quiet Moments in The Villages is her first book.